William Mac Ritchie, David Mac Ritchie

Diary of a Tour Through Great Britain in 1795

William Mac Ritchie, David Mac Ritchie

Diary of a Tour Through Great Britain in 1795

ISBN/EAN: 9783744744478

Printed in Europe, USA, Canada, Australia, Japan

Cover: Foto ©Andreas Hilbeck / pixelio.de

More available books at **www.hansebooks.com**

DIARY OF A TOUR THROUGH GREAT BRITAIN IN 1795.

BY THE

REV. WILLIAM MACRITCHIE,
MINISTER OF THE PARISH OF CLUNIE, PERTHSHIRE.

WITH AN INTRODUCTION AND NOTES
BY
DAVID MACRITCHIE,
AUTHOR OF 'THE TESTIMONY OF TRADITION,' ETC.

LONDON:
ELLIOT STOCK, 62, PATERNOSTER ROW, E.C.
1897.

INTRODUCTION.

THE writer of the following Diary was born in the parish of Clunie, Perthshire, in the year 1754, his father being a tenant-farmer in the barony of Laighwood, where his forefathers appear to have lived continuously since 1586. Presumably his earliest education was received at the parish school; but the first definite date obtainable is the 18th of February, 1772, when he matriculated as a Student in Arts of the United College of St. Salvator and St. Leonard at St. Andrews. From a long MS. poem, in which he moralizes over St. Andrews and the 'four tedious winters' he had spent there, we learn that he quitted its halls for ever on 2nd May, 1775. 'There is, however,' writes Mr. Maitland Anderson, University Librarian, 'no record of the classes he attended, and no mention of his having taken a degree. If he left St. Andrews in 1775, his Divinity course must have been taken at another University.' And indeed, while some of his writings indicate that he attended the Moral Philosophy and

Science Classes at St. Andrews, there is no special reference to Theology until the year 1777, when he was apparently present at the 'Anniversary Meeting of the Theological Society, Edinburgh.' From this there can be little doubt that he studied Divinity at the University of Edinburgh, but as the University records do not preserve the names of the theological students at that period, the inference cannot be positively verified. While at Edinburgh he also attended Professor John Walker's *Natural History* Class,[1] as is shown by his careful record of the successive lectures, sixty-seven in number, written for the most part in shorthand. Nor were his studies confined to the Universities of St. Andrews and Edinburgh, for a later note-book testifies that he was a member of Professor William Hamilton's Anatomy Class, at Glasgow University, in the session of 1782-1783. It will thus be seen that his tastes were varied and comprehensive, and in indulging these he laid in a miscellaneous stock of knowledge which unconsciously enabled him to make his Diary more attractive and interesting than it might otherwise have been.

While these scattered dates give one a fair idea of his course of study, it is not to be supposed that his time was wholly occupied in attending lectures during the long period between 1772 and 1783. One can glean something of his movements

[1] Professor Walker was appointed to the chair of Natural History in 1779.

by again turning to his collection of verse, which indicates that on leaving St. Andrews he returned to his home, where he spent the summer in pleasant rambles, botanizing, fishing, and reading his favourite poets. But a gloomier note is sounded in the verses 'On the Loss of Liberty,' written in 1776, whence it appears that for the past six months he had been engaged in some occupation, inferentially that of tutor in a family of rank, which proved so highly distasteful to him that he ends by resolving to 'be free again.' It must have been in that year, therefore, that he began his Divinity course in Edinburgh, where presumably he qualified himself for the Church. Some verses inscribed to his friend Professor Dugald Stewart, in 1782, may have been written in Edinburgh; but we have seen that he spent the winter of 1782-1783 in Glasgow. Then follows a letter, dated 'Glasgow, 24th June, 1783,' addressed to 'The Reverend The Moderator of the Presbytery of Dunkeld,' announcing his acceptance of the presentation to the living of Clunie, his native parish, which had been tendered to him by the joint patrons, 'The Duke of Atholl and the Right Honble David Ogilvy, eldest grandson of the deceased David Earl of Airly.' In Dr. Hew Scott's *Fasti Ecclesiæ Scoticanæ*, it is stated that he was licensed by the Presbytery on 11th June, 1783, and ordained on 29th April, 1784. Be this as it may, he spent the rest of his long life as minister of Clunie, of which parish he contributed a very complete description to Sir John Sinclair's *Statistical Account of Scotland* (part ix., Edinburgh, 1793, pp. 225-276). In 1795 he undertook the journey to London here chronicled; and the year 1796 was signalized by his marriage. During all his life he was a zealous student of natural phenomena, and in this connection may be cited two letters received by him from Henry Brougham, the future Lord Chancellor, who, writing as corresponding secretary of the Academy of Physics at Edinburgh, asks from the minister of Clunie a detailed contribution relating to the geology of Strathardle and the district north of Blairgowrie.[1] Mr. Brougham writes: 'We have it in contemplation to publish a volume of papers; among these it is my wish to have a clear and satisfactory account of the phenomena near your residence.' But whether this contribution was ever made, or if made, published, is unknown to the present writer. A 'Meteorological Register for the years 1821, 1822, 1823, and 1824, kept at the Manse of Clunie, Perthshire,' which appeared in the *Edinburgh Philosophical Journal* (vol. xiii., 1825), testifies also to the variety of Mr. MacRitchie's tastes; and his other memoranda show that this register was regularly kept from 1810 onward. But of all sciences, botany was his chief delight, and this is made apparent in the Diary. No other incidents in his life seem specially deserving of notice. He

[1] These letters are dated respectively 'No. 7, George Street, Edinr., Feby. 16, 1798,' and 'Edinr., June 17, 1799.'

died on 6th December, 1837, and was buried beside his kindred in the churchyard of Clunie.

With regard to the Diary itself, it may be stated that it was taken down in shorthand, as were many of his other manuscripts. It is now printed from a careful transliteration made by his son George (an uncle of the present writer), which was completed in 1842, and is entitled 'Notes of a Tour to the South, in the Year 1795.' The original Diary has disappeared. This, however, is not a matter of much moment, considering the immense care and conscientiousness of the transcriber. Nevertheless, the transcribed Diary cannot be regarded as authoritative on such a matter as the lines written by Burns on the window-pane at Rae's Inn, Moffat (p. 9, *post*). In the shorthand Diary, the vowels in 'gem' and 'granite' had obviously been omitted, and the transcriber, clearly unacquainted with the epigram, had guessed the words to be 'game' and 'grant,' which conveys little or no meaning. In the present printed copy, the words of the recognised version have been substituted. Students of Burns, therefore, will understand that the reference in the Diary is only authoritative in so far as it shows that the epigram had undoubtedly been inscribed on the window at Moffat before 26th June, 1795.

The opening portions of the Diary have already appeared in the *Scottish Antiquary* (January and April, 1896), and the greater part of the remainder in the *Antiquary* (April, 1896, to February, 1897). Its general interest will be recognised by those who read it. It concerns itself little with celebrities, but rather with everyday people and the everyday usages of the eighteenth century, and it was compiled chiefly for the diarist's own edification. To us of the closing nineteenth century it reveals a life that differs in many ways from our own; and the traveller's artless narrative has to us something of the charm of an explorer's record of journeyings in unknown lands. It would be an instructive thing if, at the end of every century, the living generation could look back upon a similar description of the ways and customs of their forefathers a hundred years before.

CONTENTS.

CHAPTER I.
From Perthshire to Edinburgh and Carlisle - - 1—18

CHAPTER II.
Kendal—The Ingleborough Caves—Lancaster - 19—36

CHAPTER III.
Preston—Liverpool—Manchester - - - - 37—52

CHAPTER IV.
Buxton and the Wonders of the Peak - - - 53—63

CHAPTER V.
Sheffield—In the Stage-Coach to London *via* Nottingham, Leicester and Northampton - - - 64—72

CHAPTER VI.
London and Windsor - - - - - - 73—100

CHAPTER VII.
Cambridge — Burleigh — Doncaster — Sheffield revisited—Leeds—Harrogate - - - - 101—118

CHAPTER VIII.

York—Castle Howard—The North Riding of Yorkshire - - - - - - - - 119—132

CHAPTER IX.

Stockton—Durham—Newcastle—Morpeth—Alnwick Castle—Chillingham and its White Cattle—The Cheviot Hills—Flodden Field—Across the Border - - - - - - - 133—154

CHAPTER X.

Kelso—Mr. William Dawson—Tweedside and its Memories—Peebles—Mid-Lothian—Return to Edinburgh - - - - - - - 155—169

CHAPTER I.

From Perthshire to Edinburgh and Carlisle.

LEAVE Clunie, Monday the 22nd June, and arrive to dinner at Perth. Dine at the King's Arms with a Lieutenant Murray, an officer of the Mankse Fencibles.[1] Have an interview with a Captain Lindsay, a respectable veteran of the navy sent hither on His Majesty's recruiting service. No seamen, he says, can be had here, though he makes them the tempting offer of twenty-five guineas a man and upwards. 'The times are hard,' says the Captain, 'and, I fear, will be harder still. We may beat the French to loggerheads by sea, if they please; but I fear we shan't be able to give *laws* to France. They will laugh at the attempt. The times are damned bad indeed, and they would never go down with

---

[1] Although the Atholl family had sold the sovereignty of the Isle of Man to the British Government in 1765, they did not relinquish all their privileges until 1829, and it is not unlikely that all the officers of the Manx Fencibles in 1795 were kinsmen of the Duke. The privates, however, were recruited in London at that date, as will be seen from a subsequent entry in the Diary (p. 98).

me at all, were it not for the help of a bottle of good claret, by ——.' It seems the Captain likes a bottle of good claret! Arrive in the evening at Kinross.

Next morning, Tuesday the 23rd, set out for the waterside. At Kelty-bridge meet a vast number of coal-drivers, who inform me they have them at the pits there at the rate of sixpence and eightpence every eighteen stone-weight. Would to God we had coals as near us, and as cheap, in the Stormont! By the side of the brooks that run by Kelty-bridge the coal appears in the face of the banks, rising even to the surface. The pits here of no considerable depth, and the coal very accessible. It is covered with a stratum of freestone, (here called a coal-band) of a considerable thickness, soft and easily wrought, but, when exposed for some time to the air, hard and durable.

A little to the North of Inverkeithing, see by the way-side the *Parietaria officinalis* and the *Juncus*—— Betwixt the turnpike and the N. Ferry observed some plants of the *Viola hirta* in the face of the basaltic rocks. Breakfast at the Ferry. No prospect of a passage till the afternoon: contrary winds and heavy rain. No matter, Cally[1] and I must not contend with the

[1] His horse; probably bought at Cally, in Strathardle. He was an Irish horse, as one learns from the elegy in which his master laments his death, some years later.

winds and the waves. Here let *Botany* afford me some consolation for the delay and the badness of the weather. Take an opportunity of a fair blink to ascend the rocks on the N.E. side of the town. Find the *Astragalus Uralensis* in flower, and also the *A. arenarius*, etc. Take off abundance of excellent specimens. Have a quick, rough passage of nine minutes, along with some of the

* * * *
'Of ancient race, in Erin first
 He drew the vital air :—
But what is ancestry to *worth*,
 Begotten when or where?
* * * *

[The elegy, which extends to twenty-six verses, concludes thus:]

'But not on Earth's infatuate orb
 Perfection can be found !
For Cally once, with all his load,
 Came stumbling to the ground!

'With all his care, he stumbled *twice;*
 (Let Truth the fact deplore)
He stumbled *thrice:*—and where's the man
 Who has not stumbled more?

'My Cally's faults were few and small;
 His virtues large we deem;
And those, when weighed in scales with these,
 Fly up, and kick the beam.

'Peace to his bones !—If brutes have souls
 (As Indian sages tell)
My Cally lives! and tastes, refined,
 The joys he loved so well.

'Avaunt ! ye snarling, critic tribe,
 Nor mock these humble lays ;
But own that Worth, in man or beast,
 Deserves the note of praise.'

King's Black Horse (Major Watson). Arrive at Edinburgh in the evening. Pass the night, next day and next night, in Edinburgh, partly for the sake of pleasure, partly for the sake of business, and principally on account of rainy weather.

Wednesday, 24th.—Dine with my cousins John and Thomas, with Principal Baird, Captain Elder, Dr. Ferguson, etc.[1] Drink tea with a Mrs. Douglass (sister of Mr. Dawson of Graden). She introduces us to her niece Mrs. Jeffrey and her husband, from Ross-shire, who are on their way to Frogden to see her father and friends, with whom I passed some happy days last summer. Part in the evening with my good friend Mr. Bruce,[2] who takes charge of my specimens of the Astragalus.

Thursday, 25th.—Leave Auld Reekie at ten o'clock a.m., and set out for Linton along the base of the Pentland Hills. Pass by Woodhouselee (Tytler Fraser, advocate). His house beautifully situated in the bosom of a cory of the mountains, commanding a fine prospect of Mid-Lothian, etc. The day hazy and murky, have

---

[1] These cousins were John MacRitchie, younger of Craigton, then practising as a 'writer' in Edinburgh, and his brother Thomas, a wine merchant in Leith; Captain Elder being their maternal uncle, a naval officer who had served under Lord Howe. Principal Baird was the Rev. Dr. George Baird, Principal of the University of Edinburgh. Dr. Ferguson may have been the eminent Professor of Moral Philosophy, Dr. Adam Ferguson.

[2] Evidently 'Mr. Arthur Bruce of the Natural History Society,' referred to in the Statistical Account of Clunie.

but an obscure prospect around me. The S. side of the Pentlands a very pleasant pastoral scene, where the *Gentle Shepherd* tends his feeding flocks. Saw, with some surprise indeed, a shepherd reclining on a green hill by the side of the way, busied in reading a *Newspaper*. ' Curse on French politics!' said I, ' for they will ruin our country. This fellow would be better employed gathering plants as I am, and at the same time taking care of his sheep. What connection has French cruelty with the happiness of this poor fellow's situation? If he has not the felicity at this moment to congratulate himself on his having been born a Scots herd, I both pity and despise him. But what business has he with that newspaper? I don't like to be uncharitable, but I cannot help thinking he puts me too much in mind of too many fine giddy girls who set their heads agog by reading romances that ought to be made a bonfire of. I like liberty as much as any man : the liberty of the press is certainly a great blessing; but alas! the very best of blessings are too often abused.'

Pass by Newhall (Brown,[1] Esq.) and enter W. Lothian.[2] Here the country abounds with good peat-moss, cast up in great quantities. See here some of the Carlock-coal, some very much impregnated with sulphur. But I never pass through

[1] In Paterson's *British Itinerary* (London, 1785) Newhall is stated to belong to ' Hay, Esq.'
[2] This is an error. Peebles is the county which here adjoins Mid-Lothian.

a coal country without feeling something like envy. Arrive at Linton a little after one o'clock, and feed Cally with good Polish oats, that is, as I was informed, oats descended from oats that were brought hither about two years ago from Poland. They are a round, firm, meaty pickle. They charge here only fourpence the lippy. The hay here one shilling a stone, owing in a great measure to their having consumed last winter an unusual quantity for the relief of their sheep.

About the division of Mid and West Lothian [*read* Mid-Lothian and Peeblesshire] there are pretty curious appearances of what we call *drums*,[1] apparently formed by currents of water. They lie at the base of the Pentlands, and run nearly parallel to the range of the mountains, or at least forming a very small angle with the range.

Set out from Linton at two o'clock, and enter Tweed-dale (county of Peebles).[2] Hamilton of Spittlehaugh on the left. Much peat-moss here; thirteen feet deep, with gravel at the bottom. Knowing Hamilton's grounds, here there is a small stratum of marle with limestone in it, and sand and different earths above it; the value of marle not understood here.

Leave the Pentlands behind me. Mendock [or Mendick] hill on my right. Pass several of the

---

[1] Although Gaelic was not the language of the Stormont in the eighteenth century, this word is really the Gaelic *druim*, a ridge.

[2] See above correction.

sources of the Tweed. Betwixt Linton and Broughton look in vain for the *Primula farinosa*, though it has certainly been found in this neighbourhood. Take up some fine plants of the *Sedum villosum*. Netherurd, Lawson, Esq.

At Broughton (property of Lord Braxfield) informed that some farms here sett at thirty shillings an acre. The mountains occupied by sheep, beautiful and green to the top. The lands in the valleys well laid out and in high culture. Blue slate quarries here. Lord Braxfield here looked upon as a miser. Proof of it: an attempt to be made for discovering coal (a thing much wanted here) was in agitation lately; and most of the substantial people here were willing to subscribe according to their abilities for defraying the expense; Lord Braxfield would not subscribe a shilling.[1]

Leave Broughton. Drummelzier (Hay, Esq.) on my left. Come into the truly pastoral banks of the Tweed, here a small river in its ordinary state, but, when swelled by the floods, it occupies the whole dale, which is here narrow, bounded by high green mountains, with a little heath intermixed near their tops. The mountains are not conical or rocky; but swell boldly from the dale, their outlines forming nearly arches of circles; rivulets winding betwixt the mountains and falling

---

[1] A somewhat hasty inference this. Lord Braxfield may have shown more wisdom than his neighbours in refusing to subscribe to this scheme.

into the Tweed in the bottom of the dale. Poolmud [Polmood], Hunter, Esq. Arrive about nine o'clock at Bield,[1] where put up all night, and sup on fresh trout from the Tweed. Tweedie of Oliver Lord of the Manor; Duke of Queensberry first Heritor.

Friday, 26th.—Leave Bield at seven o'clock a.m., and ascend the W. [or left] bank of the Tweed, which now begins to dwindle into a brook. For ten or eleven miles see no habitation of man, but two or three shepherds' huts. The whole grounds, high and low, along this tract are covered with a thin stratum of moss, in which grows bent interspersed with short heath. This tegument, which runs over even the summits of the hills, seems to be at a medium from one to three feet thick, easily cast up and forming the fuel of the inhabitants of Tweedsmuir, etc. Under this mossy covering, the whole country is gravel; the road is formed by removing the tegument. The road is excellent, though the tolls are high, twopence to Bield and all the way to Linton.

Arrive at the highest elevation of the road, where I observe plenty of the *Saxifraga stellaris,* which announces the elevation here to be very considerable, perhaps fifteen hundred feet or upwards above the level of the Solway Firth.[2] Join the Glasgow road at the head of Annandale,

---

[1] Thirty-five miles from Edinburgh; an easy day's ride.

[2] The road, which rises all the way from Bield to the watershed which divides the sources of the Tweed and the Annan, reaches at that point a height of 1,300 feet.

where fall in with my last year's tract [? track]. A little before the junction of the roads, stop and take a view of the Hartfell on my left, where I spent last year one of the happiest mornings of my life. From this elevation descend the streamlets that form the sources of the Annan on the S., the Tweed on the N., and the Clyde on the west. Mountains at the head of the Annan close in the form of a *cul-de-sac*,[1] with high, steep fronts looking towards the dale. See here the mountains of Cumberland in England. Descend to Moffat, and take up the *Jasione montana* by the way, but not in flower. Arrive at Rae's Inn to breakfast at eleven o'clock a.m.,[2] where read the following lines written on the glass in one of the windows of the room where I breakfasted :—

'*On seeing Mrs. Kemble in the character of " Yarico" at Dumfries,* 1794 :
'Kemble, thou cur'st my unbelief of Moses and his rod,
At Yarico's sweet notes of grief, the rock with tears had flow'd.
R. B.'

'*On being asked why God had made Miss Davies so small and Mrs. D—— so big:*
Ask why God made the gem so small, and why so huge the granite,
Because God meant mankind should set the higher value on it.'[3]

---

[1] The 'Devil's Beef Tub.'
[2] He had thus taken four hours to do the fourteen or fifteen miles from Bield ; a leisurely rate of progress, even considering the hilly roads and occasional pauses for botanizing.
[3] It seems probable that our traveller did not realize that 'R. B.' represented 'Robert Burns,' and that the poet him-

Company at Moffat: Lady Lockhart Ross; Mr. Irvin, West Indian; Mr. Dalzel of Glenae; Mr. Ogilvy of Chesters; Mr. Hume of Bassington [Bassindean]; Captain Lockhart, Royal Navy, son of the late Lord Covington, one of the Lords of Session; Mr. Paisley, Banker; Mr. Carruthers of Howmain, etc.

Go out to the Well and drink of the water: strong sulphur; it smells like rotten eggs, very forbidding; its taste not quite so disagreeable. It is thought good for scorbutic complaints. The Hartfell Spaw for consumptive ones. On my way to the well observed the *Symphytum officinale* and the *Jasione*.

Set out for Dumfries, and pass by Raehills, a

---

self had inscribed one, at least, of these epigrams on the window only a few months previously. A curious circumstance is that the lines on Mrs. Kemble are stated by one writer to have been written 'in Mrs. Riddel's box in the Dumfries Theatre, in the winter of 1794,' and yet the initials would lead one to believe that Burns wrote that epigram at Moffat for the first time. It is very unlikely that he would quote himself. Another noteworthy detail is that the second couplet is unsigned, although it has never been disputed that the lines were composed and written for the first time on that very spot. 'The epigram is said to have been uttered, and then inscribed on a window-pane of the principal Inn, at Moffat, on observing Miss Davies ride past in company with a lady of portly dimensions. Burns thought so well of it as to record it in the Glenriddell MS. Book, now at Liverpool.' (See *The Works of Robert Burns*, edited by William Scott Douglas. Edinburgh, W. Paterson, 1877. Vol. ii., pp. 345, 346, and vol. iii., p. 205.) It may be added that our Diary has 'Mrs. D.' instead of the accepted 'Mrs. A.,' as the initial of the stout lady. Other slight differences have already been referred to in the Introduction, p. ix.

new seat of the Earl of Hopeton. It is finely situated on the bank of the Kinnel about a mile S.W. of Lochwood, the old castle of the Annandale family. Here the Earl of Hopeton has planted a great deal of wood, and greatly embellished the face of the country, which is originally wild and mossy.

At the 10th mile-stone from Dumfries observe the following plants, viz.: *Orchis conopsea, Satyrium albidum, Athamanta Meum*; and, for the first time I ever saw it, *Genista tinctoria.*

Call upon Dr. Burgess at the Manse of Kirkmichael; the Doctor a pleasant old hospitable botanist, a correspondent of the famous Linnæus, some of whose letters are in his custody. The Doctor has the best collection of the British grasses of perhaps any British botanist. He introduces me to a Mr. Gordon, a pleasant sensible young gentleman lawyer of Dumfries, who accompanies me to Dumfries.

A little below the Manse of Kirkmichael, which is situated upon a Roman camp, I observe the *Osmunda crispa.* As we approach to Dumfries, the evening becomes very mild and pleasant; have a view of Skiddaw in Cumberland. A high mountain lies before us on the Galloway shore called Criffel (Creelfell).[1] Mr. Gordon narrates to me a curious superstitious story concerning it. Come in to Nithsdale. The country here in the highest

---

[1] The spelling 'Creelfell' is merely an invention to suit the story here alluded to, and given on pp. 14, 15 *post.*

state of culture; rich fields of potatoes, wheat, and different kinds of grain on every hand. On our left hand lies Tinwaldhouse, the seat of the Duke of Queensberry, with Tinwald Farm immediately above it, on one of the finest banks I ever saw. On our right hand lies Carnfalloch, the seat of Johnston, Esq., lately Member of Parliament for the County, etc.

After putting up our horses at the inn, Mr. Gordon walks out with me to the banks of the Nith, where we enjoy a prospect of the town; the beautifully meandering river; the ruins of Lincluden Abbey (the seat of Mr. Young on the left side of it); the whole of Nithsdale for six miles broad, and extending in length more than thirty miles to N.W., bounded on each side by delightful green mountains; the whole landscape gilded by the rays of the setting sun, and indeed one of the finest landscapes anywhere to be seen. On the opposite side of the river stand the hills of Traquair, the scene of the famous song, *The Bush aboon Traquair*.[1]

Dumfries, an elegant genteel town, containing about eight thousand inhabitants. Two bridges, the old and the new, stretch across the river and join the town to the suburbs which lie on the west side, where there is the finest set of cornmills I ever saw. The principal buildings of the town

---

[1] A misapprehension of the diarist's. The place he describes is *Troqueer*; the Traquair of the song is near Innerleithen.

are the Dumfries and Galloway Infirmary, containing an Asylum for lunatics; the Poor's House; the Correction House; the Theatre ; the Assembly Rooms ; the two Churches, and the Town Hall. In the Churchyard are a great number of beautiful monuments (one in particular belonging to the family of Hoddam), composed all of a fine freestone dug up in the neighbourhood, and executed in such a manner as plainly shows the good taste and genteel spirit of the inhabitants. No coal here; get them over from Whitehaven. Good salmon fishery. Excellent flesh-market. Before supper take a walk through the different departments of the town, which are very distinctly pointed out and explained to me by Mr. Gordon, who afterwards sups with me at the inn.

Saturday, 27th.—Set out from Dumfries at ten o'clock a.m., a delightful ride to Annan.[1] Pass through the Lockar [Lochar] Moss, and a little beyond the turnpike see again the *Genista tinctoria*. In passing over the heights betwixt Dumfries and Annan, the country has somewhat the appearance of drums[2] formed by currents. The drums point southward towards the Solway Firth, and run nearly parallel to Nithsdale. Look back from the high grounds and have a charming view of the dale from its one end to the other. Dumfries

---

[1] At Moffat, therefore, instead of keeping to the main highway leading south to Carlisle, he diverged at once to the south-west, taking the direct road from Moffat to Dumfries.

[2] Compare p. 6 *ante*.

stands about ten miles up from the Firth in the heart of the dale. From Dumfries a long ridgy eminence stretches down to the Firth, and divides the foot of the dale into two countries nearly of an equal breadth. On the west side of this ridge runs the river Nith, navigable within a mile of the town by vessels of between fifty and sixty tons. On the east side of the ridge lies Lockar Moss, stretching from ten to eleven miles towards the Firth, nearly on a level with the sea in most parts, and in some parts it is said below the sea-level. The moss[1] is of a good quality, easily cast up for fuel; and the skirts of it in some parts are very well cultivated and [produce] very good crops of oats and potatoes. The potatoes in this country are, in general, the common white potatoe, which we have in the north, and a few of the red Lancaster. Pass over the highest elevation of the road, and come down to a black, mossy part of the country.

At Hillhead (here is a great lime-work, Lady Douglas's), stop and look back on Creelfell about twenty miles west-by-south. It is the stateliest mountain in the prospect; and is perhaps not less than 3,500 feet above the Solway Firth.[2] It is vulgarly reported that the Devil, intending to form a bridge betwixt Galloway and Cumberland, had

[1] 'Moss' is here used to denote a peat-bog or moor, as in 'Chat Moss.'
[2] It is actually only 1,867 feet above the level of the sea. Its isolated position presumably increases its apparent height. Wordsworth speaks of '*huge* Criffel's hoary top.'

proceeded south thus far, forming on his way the range of mountains that bound Nithsdale on the west, and that when he had got as far as Criffle, his creel, in which he carried his stones, *fell*, and formed that vast mountain now called Creelfell (pronounced Criffle).[1] The Devil was obliged in consequence of this accident to drop his attempt, and proceeded no further in the plan of his bridge. The lands at its base are in a high state of improvement, and beautifully cultivated a great way up its sides.

On descending towards Annan have a view of Mount Annan on the left, a seat of the Marquis of Annandale. Here you see the English coast very distinctly from Wigton to Cockermouth and Whitehaven; with the high mountains on each side of the Bassenthwaite Lake; and, between these, the summits of the mountains beyond Keswick and the Derwentwater.

Annan, an elegant little cleanly town, beautifully situated on the E. bank of the Annan, over which there is a good old bridge. From the bridge you have a fine prospect up Annandale, with the windings of the river; but the view is inferior to that at Dumfries. Annan about nine miles from the Firth, following the course of the river. A salmon fishery and good cotton manufactory. Victual here in this country all sold by weight, seventeen and a half pounds the stone: other articles, wool,

---

[1] An etymology analogous to that which derives 'Guthrie from the royal command to 'gut three' (herrings).

etc., fourteen pounds per stone. Meal here sold at present at twenty-six pence the stone-weight. There is a windmill[1] here for grinding wheat, etc. At a small village betwixt Annan and Gretna, on a sign-post above the door of a small alehouse is painted a gate with this inscription under it:

> 'This gate hangs well and hinders none;
> Refresh and pay, and travel on.'

A little farther on, above the door of another small alehouse, are written these words:

> 'Bread, beer,
> Sold here.'

The Borderers seem to be fond of rhiming. Such trifles as these sometimes catch the eye of a solitary traveller. Have a fine view of Mossknowe, the seat of Captain Græme of Dumfries, on the left hand. Arrive at the famous Gretna-green (Mrs. Howe), and dine sumptuously in one of the pleasantest inns in the kingdom, where so many fond lovers have had their hearts and their fortunes united by Pasley, of whom I here find the following lines pencilled on one of the window-shutters in the room where I dine:

> 'Old Pasley the priest, who does lovers unite,
> Is stiled by the wise ones an old Gretna Bite;
> To be sure 'tis for money he follows the trade;
> No woman possessing it should die an old maid.'[2]

---

[1] Windmills were, and are, rarities in Scotland.

[2] The following appeared in *Notes and Queries* (Series VIII., ix., January 25, 1896):

'Joseph Pasley acquired a good business. He obtained the name of the Old Blacksmith, probably on account of the

The motto of the armorial bearings above the door of Gretna-hall is *cave paratus*, not an improper caveat perhaps for a bridegroom just about to be *matrimonized*. After leaving Gretna, instead of going by Longtown, as last year, take the short road to Carlisle by the sands; enter on English ground again, and get safely across the river Esk. On the south bank of the river, opposite the fording-place, there is a little public-house with this motto on the sign-post:

> 'Gentlemen here take a guide,
> To either Scotch or English side,
> And have no cause to fear the tide.'

Betwixt the river Esk and Carlisle have an agreeable ride along the east bank of the river Eden. See here the *Plantago media, Sambucus Ebulus, Jasione montana, Valeriana Locusta, Galium Mollugo*, etc.

The approach to Carlisle from the north-west is most pleasant of any. The river Eden divides into two branches immediately to the north of the

---

mythological conceit of Vulcan being employed in riveting the hymeneal chains. Pasley was at first a smuggler, a farmer, and a fisherman, then a tobacconist, but never at any time a blacksmith. His first residence was at Megg's Hill, on the common or green between Gretna and Springfield, to the last of which villages he removed in 1782. He commenced his public career about 1753, and at first gave certificates signed with a feigned name. Latterly he took to wearing canonicals, and attached his real signature to the marriage certificates. He was a great drinker, and at his decease, in January, 1811, aged eighty-four, weighed twenty-five stone.'

He was of the same family as General Pasley (*Notes ana Queries*, February 22, 1896).

town; the branch next the town passes under a bridge of seven, and the branch farthest off passes under a bridge of four arches; the two branches upon their union make a long magnificent winding, which embraces an extensive plain. On the southeast side of this peninsula stands the Castle, under a considerable elevation. To the left of the Castle you see the Cathedral, with its noble square tower. To the left of the Cathedral you see the town, the bridges, and the river winding under your feet; in the middle-ground a finely-cultivated country along the banks of the river; and in the background the Cumbrian mountains elevating their lofty tops to the sky. Put up all night at Sowerby's.

CHAPTER II.

Kendal—The Ingleborough Caves—Lancaster.

SUNDAY, 28th.—Get up at five by the sound of the trumpet and join the 30th Regiment of Dragoons (Ulster Light Dragoons) on their route to Birmingham, ordered up there for the purpose of quelling the riots. Enter into conversation with a Captain Armstrong and a Lieutenant Newton, both gentlemen of Ireland; and march along with them to Penrith, where arrive to breakfast; put up at Buchannan's (Walmsley), one of the first inns in the North of England. It was not finished when I was here last year on my way to the Lakes. Here meet and get acquainted with a Mr. Cameron, from Glasgow. Prince William of Gloucester[1] arrives on his way to Keswick;

[1] This was George III.'s brother, William Henry, created Duke of Gloucester and Edinburgh in 1764. From an entry in the *Scots Magazine* of 1795 (p. 408), it appears that Prince William had spent the previous Monday and Tuesday in Edinburgh, that he had thereafter visited Hopetoun House, the Carron Works, ' the Great Canal,' and finally Glasgow, and that he was now on his way 'to join the camp near Newcastle.' This last statement does not agree with the state-

and here for the first time I have the honour of seeing one of the Royal Family. A Lord Valentia from Ireland follows his Highness.[1] Dine with Mr. Cameron, who gives me letters of recommendation to some of his friends in Lancaster. After dinner (at dinner we had potatoes of this year, above the size of gun-bullets) set out for Shap, by Lord Lonsdale's, a fine place on the right hand.[2] Much old oak, which his Lordship will by no means cut down; a fine fallow-deer park; feeds much cattle and horses. Has a few red deer at a distance from the house near the fells (red deer in Martindale by the Ulswater Lake, but now few in number); parted with his lady; keeps a great number of servants here; his estate managed by two stewards, an upper and [an] under one; pass by his whimsical, half-finished, never-inhabited village.[3] Arrive in the evening at Shap,[4] a small village high up in the country. Walk into the churchyard, where see the *Plantago media* in great abundance. (Here, again, I tasted potatoes of this year's growth, as big, or bigger, than a pigeon's egg.) This village had formerly a good market for cattle, corn, and butter; but the

---

ment in the Diary, that he was on his way to Keswick; but probably this discrepancy could be accounted for.

[1] Arthur, Viscount Valentia (of the Annesley family), who was created Earl of Mountnorris in 1793 (*Burke*).

[2] Lowther Hall, now Lowther Castle.

[3] Marked 'New Village' in Paterson's *Itinerary*.

[4] Nine or ten miles from Penrith, a short evening's ride; in marked contrast to the eighteen miles from Carlisle to Penrith, performed before breakfast.

market has lately fallen off; the neighbourhood abounds in good pasture; remarkable for good hay.

Monday, 29*th*.—Rainy morning; detained here till after seven o'clock, when set out for Kendal across the Fells—a long, hilly road.[1] Find for the first time the *Primula farinosa* in moist, swampy grounds on the side of the Fells about half-way betwixt Shap and Kendal. Meet here Lord Darlington's dragoons on their march to Penrith, mounted on fine bay horses, and dressed in scarlet cloaks with yellow necks. About three miles north of Kendal have a fine view of the town with its environs. See here at a distance to the right the lofty mountains about the head of the Coningston and Windermere waters; on the left the mountains towards the West Riding of Yorkshire. Arrive at Kendal[2] about eleven o'clock, and breakfast at the White Hart (Maskew's). After breakfast walk up on the west side of the town to the Obelisk, erected in 1788 in memory of the Revolution in 1688, and sacred to *Liberty*. Have here a beautiful prospect of the town, consisting principally of one street, and the Castle on the other side. Near the south end of the town stands the church, by the west bank of the river, an elegant building with a square tower and a fine chime of bells, with the vicarage-house in its neighbourhood. The river Kent winds down

[1] This, however, was the main western highroad.
[2] A distance of fifteen miles from Shap.

the east side of the town, watering the bottom of a pleasant, fruitful, well-cultivated country. The shops in Kendal are, some of them, very magnificent. The houses generally two stories high, and each house inhabited by one family. The population of the place supposed to be about 5,000.[1] This place famous for its manufactures of woollen cloth, etc. Leave the White Hart and proceed to Kirkby-Lonsdale. Have a delightful ride to the seventh milestone from Kendal; here turn to the left[2] up a romantic little valley to the north of Farlton Knot. This mountain is celebrated by tourists as remarkably similar to the rock of Gibraltar, and it is composed entirely of limestone. On the way to Kirkby-Lonsdale, I observed a great deal of the *Betonica officinalis* growing by the waysides, also some plants of the *Jasione*, etc. (*Arum maculatum* at the root of the hedges); and on the walls on each side of the entrance to Kirkby-Lonsdale I saw the *Sedum reflexum*. At Kirkby-Lonsdale put up at the Royal Oak (Rawlinson). Take a walk to the churchyard; view the parsonage, a very neat one indeed; proceed up the west bank of the river Lune, along a beautiful gravel-walk, till come to a resting-seat, where have one of the most enchanting prospects in nature. Casterton Hall opposite, a new elegant seat of Wilson, Esq.; nothing can exceed it in point of situation. The bank where you here sit is very steep and high;

[1] In 1891 the population was 14,430.
[2] The main road continuing south by Burton to Lancaster.

the Lune makes an admirable meander under your feet, and glides in an easy serpentine course down to the bridge (said to have been built by the Devil; but the Devil never built such a bridge in all his life, and ignorant, superstitious people everywhere give him more credit than is due to him). Kirkby - Lonsdale, a pleasant summer village as any in England, but cold and damp in winter, on account of its situation being high up near the mountains. (Plenty of coal from the neighbourhood, and lime.) It contains about a thousand or from that to twelve hundred people. No considerable manufacture; a good many shoes and boots made here. About a mile and a half below the town is Overborough (Fenwick, Esq., deceased), a place of very considerable beauties. Proceed east from Kirkby-Lonsdale six miles to Thornton Church Stile, Yorkshire, within four miles of Yordas Cave. The bold shoulders of Ingleborough now appear before me; but alas! his head is wrapt up in clouds. Put up all night at Brown's, however, in hopes of a fair day to-morrow; have at supper remarkably delicious trouts from the Kingsdale river that runs hard by. A heavy rain begins to fall in the evening, which threatens a bad day to-morrow.

Tuesday, 30th.—The mountains all enveloped in mist, the brooks swelled, and the rain still continuing. Rest in bed till eight o'clock; get up, and breakfast at nine on coffee. Look out with impatience for fair weather; no interval of the rain at mid-day. Dreary disappointment this: yet the traveller through life must sometimes meet with disappointments. Amuse myself the best way I can within doors: dry my plant-books; and shift my plants. About one p.m. the clouds disperse, and the sun appears. Take a guide, tinder, candles, provisions; mount horses and ascend towards Yordas Cave. On our way have a very striking view of Thornton-force Cascade,[1] the grandeur of which much enhanced by the recent rains. The fall of the Kingsdale river here about thirty yards. From the rocks on each side, particularly on the left side of the Great Fall, small streams descend from nearly the same height with the great one, all tumbling with tremendous roar into the gulph below, from which the spray unceasingly ascends. This Fall much more astonishing than any I had seen last summer among the lakes of Cumberland, etc. It is not inferior, at least in time of floods, to the Fall of Foyers, Inverness-shire. Ascending from Thornton-force Cascade, we come next to Keldshead. Here the river Kingsdale issues in a broad, deep, black fountain, perhaps not less than twenty yards broad, from the base of the mountain Gragareth. A stream of such magnitude as this springing at once from the foot of a great mountain must strike every stranger with equal surprise

---

[1] It may safely be assumed that the superfluous 'Cascade' is an addition of the diarist's, who was evidently not aware that 'Force' had the same meaning.

and astonishment. Ascend to the head of the dale, and come near the entrance of the Cave at the northwest corner of the dale, immediately under the base of the mountain. Enclose our horses in the sheepfolds. A shepherd joins us at the folds, and accompanies us into the Cave. Each carries a light in one hand and a staff to assist our steps in the other. Enter the Cave and quit the light of day. Large torrents of water roar down through the bottom of the Cave, increasing the horrors of the scene; pass through several currents wading up to the knees; come into the centre of the most magnificent dome I ever saw or probably ever will see upon the face of the earth. Its length seems to be about seventy or eighty yards; but its height no one can tell. I threw up a small stone with all my might, which after a considerable interval of time fell beside us; but when I asked the guides if they thought it struck the roof, they laughed at the idea. It must be upwards of a hundred feet high. After scrambling over rocks, and wading sometimes in deep water, where to me every step seemed big with danger, we got up at last to what is called the Chapter-house, on the northwest side of the Cave, from its having some fanciful resemblance to a Chapter-house. Here the rocks are worn by the water into the most grotesque forms, and petrifactions of different kinds appear all around; indescribably great! After passing about half an hour in the Cave, we returned slowly to the light of day; brought off some specimens of the minerals of the Cave. The plants I observed about the rocks at the entrance of Yordas are *Saxifraga tridactylites, Asplenium Scolopendrium, Stellaria nemorum, Polypodium fragile*, etc.

After leaving Yordas, ascend the mountain and come to Pool-pot-hole, and still higher up to Gingling Cave, where there is good marble with entrochi intermixed. There are deep gullies in the mountain, so narrow in some places that one might almost leap over from one side to the other; but he would be a bold adventurer indeed that would attempt it, for the deep below has not in some places been yet fathomed; and to look down into these pits is truly tremendous. We threw down stones into Gingling Cave, and heard them tumbling from rock to rock for the space of several seconds; sometimes loud and sometimes lower, till at last the sound died away, nor could we tell whether they reached the bottom or not.

Return along the steep side of Gragareth down to Keldshead, and taking a route different from what we took in ascending the mountain, we arrived in the evening at Thornton Church Stile.

Wednesday, 1st July.—Fine morning: rise at five and set out with my guide for Chapel-in-the-dale. Having taken lights and provisions along with us; pass through the village of Ingleton, where there is a cotton-mill not in a very thriving condition.

Large coal pits in the neighbourhood. Fine blue slate quarries, with pyrites and arboreous impressions in some of the veins very remarkable. Travel for some miles along the base of Ingleborough, composed of limestone, except in a few places where the veins of the schistus run across. The strata of the slate in this neighbourhood are all nearly vertical. The coal is from forty to sixty yards deep, covered with a soft grit; the coal-strata dip all to the North. The limestone upon the base of Ingleborough, and over all the scars and mountains here, appears upon the very surface without any sort of superincumbent vegetable mould. It exhibits everywhere around a most singular appearance, rising tier above tier like the steps of a stair; the tiers running round the mountains and scars all nearly in a horizontal direction; each tier is cut perpendicularly by a thousand fissures; and in stepping along these horizontal layers of limestone, you find them all perforated like a honey-comb, and at each step you are in danger (unless you walk very circumspectly) of falling down into these crevises, and breaking your bones. In some places the holes are large and almost unfathomably deep.—Such is the general appearance of the mountains over all this country.

After leaving the lime-quarries of Ingleton, we proceed upwards for four miles along the Dale, the immense base of Ingleborough towering on our right hand, and Twisleton Scar on our left, the river Greta running down the vale betwixt them. A little below the Chapel come to God's-bridge, where the whole river is concealed for upwards of seventy yards under a limestone rock that runs across it in horizontal columns. Come to Chapel-in-the-dale, where put up our horses, and call upon the Curate (Mr. Elishaw) a very sensible and worthy man. After drinking some rum and water with him in his house, walk out in his company to Hurtle-pot. It gives one exactly the idea of the Avernian Lake as described by Virgil. The curate leads us next to Weather-coate Cave, a little higher up. This the most astonishing fall of water I have yet seen; about sixty yards high; falling into a profound basin, on the side of which you go down for hundreds of feet through rude over-arching rocks, that threaten to bury you in your descent. At last you come to a place where you can stand in safety and view the cascade. A prodigious stream falls in front from a subterraneous passage, from which it issues with an amazing projectile force, which shows that it must have a very considerable descent before it makes its appearance in daylight. On the left-hand side of the Cave, another stream of less magnitude falls perpendicularly into the basin through a hole of the rock resembling the chimney of some lofty edifice in ruins. On the right hand, several little very striking streams pour out of holes in the rock apparently about the size of the mouths of large cannons: these streamlets fall in beautiful cascades from the height of at least one hundred and twenty feet; and all these pour into the great basin which lies about fifty feet below you, and from which the spray ascends so thick as to wet one to the skin in a few minutes. In time of sunshine there appears above the basin the most striking rainbow that can possibly be conceived. In very dry weather a person may descend to the margin of the water, and even venture round its edge. On your left hand, that is on the west side of the basin, there is a subterranean passage communicating far and wide below the rock; but which is at present inaccessible by reason of the floods. In very high floods, that is perhaps once in seven years, the whole cave is filled to the height of more than two hundred feet and overflows atop.—Ascend through the over-arching rocks with cautious steps guided by the curate. On the left hand as you ascend there is a most curious cavern scooped out by the waters in the most grotesque form, called the Fairies' Hall, where the rocks are incrusted with icicles[1] and stalactites of every figure that fancy can form.

Leaving Weathercoate Cave, ascend some hundred yards by the side of the Greta and see Ginglepot Cave. Here the river, as at Weathercoate, sinks and entirely disappears in the rocks. The depth of this cave is not known; a stone

[1] It is, of course, evident that the diarist does not intend the word 'icicle' to be understood in its literal sense.

thrown down makes a gingling noise for a long time till the noise ceases to be heard in the vast profound. Some adventurous persons, we were told by the curate, had let themselves be towed down by ropes to the depth of several hundred feet but saw no bottom; the Cave penetrated downwards to the north they could not say how far.

Next proceed about a mile up the Dale towards the base of Whernside (the highest mountain in South Britain).[1] Here come to Gatekirk Cave; and enter at the upper end of it, conducted by our good friend the curate, he leading the way with one torch in his hand, I following him with another, and my guide last of all with a third. Proceed downwards over broken rocks, and by the side of water-falls; the whole river Greta passes underground here for the space of about a hundred yards. Descend by the sides of the stream, sometimes wading, sometimes scrambling, sometimes creeping. The river divides into two branches in the middle of the Cave, that form a sort of island, composed of the most amazing petrifactions: Here we strike off some specimens. Descend till we come at last in sight of the light of day, which appears to us like fire seen at a distance; could not possibly have access to it on

---

[1] This statement was probably made by the guide, and accepted without question as correct. It is scarcely necessary to point out that Whernside (2,415 feet) is surpassed by many of the mountains of North-Western England—not to speak of Snowdon and other Welsh mountains.

account of the falls and swell of the river.—Return upwards by a different route, guided with very great dexterity and friendly attention by Mr. Elishaw. Arrive at last in the upper regions; and congratulating ourselves on having arrived there in safety, we recline on the rocks at the entrance of the Cave and refresh ourselves with a bumper of rum shrub. Descend above-ground to the place where the river issues out of the Cave; look in there and have an awful view of that end of the Cave.

After this we travel about a mile and a half to the south, and ascend to Douk Cave, situated in the face of the base of Ingleborough on the north side. The Cave is open atop as well as Weathercoate. It seems to be about one hundred yards long by about seventy broad, of an elliptical figure, and the rock about a hundred feet high. On the north side we got with some difficulty to the bottom and travelled to the south end of the cavity, where a large stream of water pours about thirty feet from the rock above through a large aperture. In dry weather, the curate told us, he had ascended into this aperture, and travelled for at least half a mile under the base of the mountain without coming to an end.

Having ascended from this immense cavity with cautious steps and slow, we here parted with our worthy friend Mr. Elishaw, and ascended to the summit of Ingleborough, where we enjoyed one of the most extensive and wonderful prospects in the world. We dined on the summit of the mountain, the clouds rolling in awful forms under our feet, and sometimes suddenly wrapping us up in darkness. Sometimes, however, it as suddenly dispelled; and gave us a glimpse of the sea extending from the Welch mountains on the left hand north to the mountains of Cumberland, &c., on the right; the whole country of Lancashire, with its rivers, towns and villages, &c., lying in extensive map below us. The town of Lancaster, though at the distance of at least twenty-four miles in a straight line, appeared at the base of the mountain; and the fells and scars that seemed high mountains to us as we ascended the valley, now appeared on the level of the plain.

In descending the mountain, the traveller cannot help remarking a vast number of curious conical holes with their apex inverted, all round the base of the mountain, some of them of a very considerable diameter and depth. Such phenomena are observable about the base of Mount Ætna in Sicily.—Arrive at Chapel-in-the-Dale about five o'clock p.m.; took our horses and set out for a few miles along the road that leads to Richmond. Stop at Gearstones, a little beyond the source of the Ribble: go about half a mile south, and with two guides enter Catknot Hole. Here we perform by far the longest subterranean expedition we have attempted; through rocks and deep water, sometimes carried on the back of one of my guides, and sometimes obliged to wade myself up to the top of my boots,[1] we penetrate upwards for the space of not less, we supposed, than half-a-mile. The Cave is narrow all the way; and the height, which at the entrance is considerable, diminishes as you proceed inwards. The Cave takes several windings in its course; the petrifactions on all hands are numerous and curiously diversified. The icicles depend in the most astonishing forms from the roof and sides of the Cave; spars, crystals and incrustations of various kinds appear by the light of our candles bright as alabaster itself. In some places they assume the appearances of men and different animals in different attitudes and postures; in others they appear like swine and carcases of beef and mutton hung up on shambles; in others they resemble guns and swords, and other warlike instruments. In some places where the roof was so low as to be distinctly illuminated by our candles, we could see the ceiling stretching over us horizontally like the ceiling of some magnificent dome, most admirably sculptured and decorated by human art. The vast variety of astonishing objects that occurred as we advanced, completely alleviated our fatigue, and as completely overcame every idea of danger. As we proceeded one after another (at the bottom) our voices resounded in solemn tones from the distant recesses of the cavities. The idea of a chorus struck us. I desired the guides from time to time to hollow

[1] Long riding-boots, of course.

out on different notes of the scale, which I accompanied the best way I could, striking chords or base-notes.

> 'Here through the long-drawn aisle and fretted vault.
> The pealing anthem swell'd the notes of praise.'

Never was echo heard to greater advantage than in this indescribable recess. When we had proceeded so far that the roof became so low as to prevent us from walking upright, we found our candles half exhausted, and then it was necessary for me to sound a retreat. On our return we stopped at different places, and took off with a hammer most curious specimens of the crystallizations, etc., of this wonderful place; and having passed about an hour and a half under ground we emerged again to the light of day.

Having thus visited Catknot Hole, my curiosity with regard to Caves was fully gratified. We returned to Gearstones, where I got my boots emptied of water and dried; and having put on dry stockings, and refreshed ourselves in the public-house, we mounted horses and rode down the dale in the evening to Ingleton.

Thursday, 2nd July.—Went to the Slate-quarries and got good specimens of the pyritical and dendritical slate. Went also a-botanizing through the romantic dens and woods and precipices above Ingleton. There and among the mountains and caves of this wonderful country, I observed the following rare plants: viz., *Convallaria majalis* in great plenty; *Convallaria multiflora* ; *Ophrys muscifera* ; *Satyrium viride* and *S. albidum ;* *Primula farinosa* ; *Serapias latifolia* ; *Ophioglossum vulgatum;* *Saxifraga tridactylitis;* *Saxifraga aizoides* and *S. hypnoides* ; *Asplenium Scolopendrium* and *A. viride;* *Valeriana dioica;* *Arum maculatum;* *Orchis canopsea* ; *Genista tinctoria;* *Schœnus nigricans;* *Ophrys ovata* ; *Polypodium fragile* ; *Stellaria nemorum* ; *Cochlearia officinalis* ; *Draba incana* ; *Vaccinium occycoccus;* &c. &c. ; besides a great many plants not come into flower. I did not find the *Cypripedium,* nor the *Ophrys apifera,* but got a plant of both from a garden in the neighbourhood. *Sanguisorba officinalis;* *Plantago media;* *Betonica officinalis;* &c.

Friday, 3rd July.—Pack up my plants and minerals and leave them to the care of the landlord to be forwarded to Edinburgh. Set out in the afternoon for Lancaster, a delightful ride by Hornby, etc., where arrive about eight p.m.[1] Take a guide and go up to the Castle, as well worth the seeing as anything of the kind I have ever seen. The new apartments for the State prisoners lately erected by Harrison on a plan that would highly please the benevolent Howard himself. Sixty-four neat apartments for them, with enclosed ground without for air and exercise. Go up to John of Gaunt's Tower, and enjoy an amazingly fine prospect of the town, the bridge, the windings of the Lune, the sea, and the dis-

[1] A ride of twelve or fourteen miles.

tant mountains, etc. Put up at the King's Arms (Coulthwaite), and sup with a Mr. Lapworth from Coventry.

Saturday, 4th July.—Deliver my letters to Mr. Tinning, who very kindly invites me to dinner, and walks out with me through the town, by the shore, etc. Shows me the shipping; explains the genius of the people, and introduces me at dinner to some gentlemen of fortune and influence in the place; a Mr. Clarkson (Controuler of the Customs); his cousin Clarkson, Rector of ——, in the neighbourhood, who lately married a lady of fortune, and who forsooth keeps his hounds and his horses; a Mr. Ashton, brother to a gentleman of three thousand pounds a year in Yorkshire, etc. After dinner go to the Play. Mrs. Siddons in the character of Lady Macbeth; her brother Kemble plays Macbeth. The representation very tolerable upon the whole, though Mrs. Siddons be poorly supported. Mrs. Siddons's Benefit. A brilliant audience; the Lancashire ladies in all their charms. After the Play, return to supper at Mr. Tinning's. Here introduced to a Mr. Stuart (of Appin) a Scotchman.[1] After supper, at the table of a kind, hospitable landlord, return to the King's Arms, and enjoy four hours of slumber.

[1] This casual reference seems inadequate after the glowing words in which Hogg, the Ettrick Shepherd, laments the decay of the once famous Stewarts of Appin.

CHAPTER III.

Preston—Liverpool—Manchester.

SUNDAY, 5th July.—Set out from the King's Arms at eight in the morning, musing on my own people and the duties I owe them. Cannot man be devout in the fields, said I, as well as in the pulpit?

Canal forty-five miles upon a level (no locks till beyond Preston) to join the Duke of Bridgewater['s]. About five miles south of Lancaster enjoy one of the noblest of prospects. To the west-by-north Peel Castle, and beyond it a little to the left the summits of the mountains in the Isle of Man. Beyond [behind] me the mountains of the highlands of Lancashire, Cumberland, etc., far seen to the north and north-west dim in the clouds. To the west the boundless expanse of the ocean, with ships gliding with gentle breezes over its surface. Betwixt me and the ocean an amazing extent of the levellest country I ever saw, all enclosed and subdivided and sheltered with wood, interspersed with fine grass parks[1] (for in Lancaster [Lancashire] they have little corn), with neat houses and gentlemen's seats as far as the eye can penetrate. Black Pool about sixteen miles on my right towards the shore. Informed the company are not yet all come to the sea-bathing.

Arrive at Garstang[2] to breakfast. Betwixt Garstang and Preston, pass by on my left Clyton [Claughton] Hall and Berton [Barton] Lodge; eminent country seats of eminent esquires. Come towards Preston[3] to dinner. Six windmills here for grinding corn. Preston a larger town than Lancaster; neat streets, and fine walks. Cotton manufacture the principal one here. *Preston.* Dine at the Bull. After dinner walk out to the banks of the Ribble, here a stately navigable stream; last week I had seen it at its source, rising out of the mountains of the West Riding of Yorkshire, a *fountain* only a few yards broad. Preston a beautiful town, built all of brick made in its neighbourhood. The walk on the south side of the town, and the prospect from it, are exceedingly delightful. Walton Hall, Sir Harry Aiton's; Frenchwood, Mr. Starkey's. On the right, the late Mr. Parker's, Sheriff of the County; five miles further on the right, Aughton Tower, the residence of King James II.; Tuckworth

[1] In Scotland 'park' denotes any enclosed meadow or pasture, however small. It is evidently in this sense that it is used above.
[2] Ten miles from Lancaster.
[3] Eleven miles from Garstang.

Hall, the seat of Mr. Rosteram; Penwortham, the seat of Mr. Barton. Earl Derby lord of the manor. His Lordship in opposition to the present Ministry. Unpopular here. The Races (which continue for three days annually here) come on about the middle of this month. His Lordship then expected down here; and soon after that a hot election. Two superb rooms in the Black Bull; the one for dining great company, the other for private assemblies, etc. A good assortment of bedrooms.

Leave Preston at five p.m., and proceed to Ormskirk, eighteen miles. Pass the Ribble below the town. The river here runs under a good bridge of five arches. Have a pleasant afternoon ride. England now begins to assume a richer and more inland appearance. The country flat and beautiful all the way to Liverpool. Perfectly like a great well-cultivated garden all round. Rich fields begin now to appear of wheat and barley in the ear; good oats and beans in the blossom; potatoes also in the flower. The *Pink-eye* potatoe, as it is here called, is becoming the fashionable potatoe of this country; it is preferred to the *Champion*.

In passing along the public roads in this country one cannot help remarking the good breeding of the people, displayed even in their children. You never meet a country person here, young or old, but salutes you with a bow or a curtsey, and a 'good-morrow,' if it be in the forenoon, and a 'good-night,' if it be late in the afternoon or towards evening.

The women of Lancashire seem to be in general, of an agreeable person, a remarkably good look, and a sound, healthy constitution. They have something *bewitching*[1] about them, indeed; but many of the first looking country girls wear black stockings on the week-days, which is by no means an improvement to their charms.

Betwixt Preston and Ormskirk I observed the *Sisymbrium amphibium*, and, for the first time in its native seat, the *Butomus umbellatus*. About five miles north of Ormskirk, and in stagnant old ditches by the wayside in that neighbourhood, I found the *Hottonia*. Arrive in the evening at Burscobridge,[2] on the bank of the Wigan Canal. This Canal from Wigan to Liverpool is about thirty-five miles; its superficial breadth is about thirty-five feet; its bottom breadth is about twenty-five; and its depth about five and a half. Earl Derby lord of the manor here. Put up all night at Abram's.

---

[1] An obvious allusion to *The Lancashire Witches*. It is interesting to add that Mrs. Grant of Laggan, writing in 1803, uses similar terms. 'What pleased me most,' she says, 'was the distinguished beauty of the Lancastrian women, not void of the more attractive charms of grace and softness' (*Letters from the Mountains*, vol. iii., Letter XL.).

[2] Burscough Bridge, three miles north-north-east of Ormskirk. As he halted here for the night (probably for the sake of his horse), instead of carrying out his intention of going on to Ormskirk, his day's ride amounted to thirty-six miles.

Monday, 6th July.—Set out after breakfast for Liverpool. Pass through Ormskirk, a considerable town with four neat streets meeting at the cross, and there forming right angles. At the church there is a venerable old square tower, and a steeple with a spire adjoining. Bells ring constantly in England. Betwixt Ormskirk and Liverpool have a view of the mountains of Wales beyond the Dee. Observe by the wayside, on this track, the following plants, viz.: *Jasione montana, Iberis nudicaulis, Hottonia lacustris, Geranium cicutarium, Sium angustifolium, Nymphœa lutea, Œnanthe crocata*, etc. The crop here looks very promising. The oats, and wheat, and barley all in the ear; large fields of potatoes very well dressed, and country girls, with their petticoats tucked up, bestriding the drills and taking out every weed with their hands. The Pink-eye cultivated here. Taking up the potatoes here already of a very considerable size and carrying them to market.

The day becomes intolerably hot; stop at the public-house about six miles north of Liverpool, and refresh Cally and myself. Approach to Liverpool from the northwest. Vast number of ships under sail making their way out of the river. Put up at the Cross Keys near the Exchange, where dine; after dinner call upon Mr. Keay,[1]

---

[1] This gentleman was presumably a native of the traveller's own part of Perthshire, where that surname is one of old standing.

and take the grace-drink with him. In the evening Mr. Keay accompanies me out, and shows me the docks and the shipping. This infinitely the most wonderful scene of the kind I have ever seen; and one who has not seen it cannot possibly conceive any idea of it. Sup at the Cross Keys (Mrs. Walker) with a number of travelling gentlemen; some of them very entertaining; Welch, Irish, English, Scotch, American, West Indies—variety of characters.

Tuesday, 7th July. Liverpool.—Call at Mr. Keay's to breakfast. After breakfast walk out through the lanes and streets of this extensive and opulent town. The streets are by no means wide or elegant, a few excepted—Castle Street, etc. Few elegant squares, as in Edinburgh. The houses here, except the outer crust of the Exchange, which was lately burnt, the churches, and the doors and windows of most of the better sort of houses, are all built of brick, have a light appearance, but seem to be by no means substantial buildings. The houses in general are three stories high and a sunk story; Castle Street four stories. The churches are elegant, except St. Paul's (clumsy imitation of); and the spires of some of them lofty, light, and easy—St. Thomas's remarkably so. The population of the place supposed to be from sixty to seventy thousand.[1] But Liverpool probably covers much

[1] The population of Liverpool, not including Birkenhead, was 39,000 in 1781, and 85,300 in 1801. At the census of

more ground than Edinburgh, though the houses are not nearly so high, nor inhabited each by so many different families.

Take a walk up Duke's Street to Mount Pleasant, the finest walk here I ever yet set a foot on, and enjoying one of the most striking prospects—the town, the river, the shipping, the opposite coast of Cheshire, the summits of the Welch mountains, etc. Visit the Infirmary. In the afternoon take a particular view of the different streets and lanes, which, in general, are narrow and dirty. Visit again the greatest thing to be seen here, or perhaps anywhere else—the Docks. Storehouses, the largest of any in Britain —particularly the Duke of Bridgewater's, etc. One gentleman here has storehouses eleven stories high. Bathing-houses, ladies' and gentlemen's; coffee-rooms; vast number of windmills for grinding corn, flint for the potteries, flax-seed for oil, log-wood, etc.

Liverpool lies from north-by-west to south-by-east nearly, on a gentle-rising ground on the east bank of the Mersey, which is about one and a half miles broad opposite the town. The docks extend more than one and a half miles, and exceed all description. This war, however, has considerably affected the trade of Liverpool. Harbour difficult of access, the tract in the river

---

1891 the figures were : Liverpool, 517,980 ; Birkenhead, 99,857—together, 617,837.

narrow, and many sand-banks on each side; pilots necessary.

Wednesday, 8th July. Liverpool.—The town crowded with the weekly [semi-weekly] market, which is held on Wednesday and Saturday. Visit Mr. Keay, who amuses me with a sight of Macklin's Bible. This is the greatest work of the kind ever attempted in Britain. The paper, the type, and the engraving superb and striking in the highest degree. The price of the copy to subscribers will be about forty guineas, in numbers. Each number contains one engraving of some of the most-affecting passages of Holy Writ, besides a number of beautiful vignettes here and there interspersed through the work. The most eminent Masters of the kingdom are employed in this work, which certainly does honour to the country. It is dedicated to the King. Walk out again to the Docks. The Glasshouse here upon a small scale. The Copper work discontinued here; removed to Wales on account of the nearness of the ore there. Number of the best ships belonging to this place taken during the present war. Ships of upwards of a thousand tons built here—

'An endless grove of masts!'

It gives one a very high idea indeed of the immense trade of Liverpool, supposed superior to that of Bristol, and inferior only to that of London.

Dine with Mr. Keay. He has earned by honest industry a very independent fortune, and lives sumptuously; supposed to be worth twenty-five thousand pounds; is getting an elegant house fitted up for himself in the skirts of the town, and is going to retire from business. Introduced at his house to Mrs. Burton, to her father, Mr. Banner, Mr. Colshaw, etc. In the afternoon visit in company the gentlemen's and ladies' bathing-rooms, constructed upon an excellent and most convenient plan—are said to be the best of any in England. Afterwards visit the Fort commanding the entrance of the river; strong, and well accommodated with ordnance for defence. Thence go up by the Cotton Mills, see the Prisons, visit the porter brewery—said to be upon a larger scale than Whitbread's, or any of the London works of the kind. Go up to Averton [? Everton] and eat fruit; noble prospect here. Come down in the evening, and sup at Mrs. Burton's. Return after supper with Mr. Keay to town, and take my leave of him, determined to set out for Manchester to-morrow.

Thursday, 9th July.—Breakfast at the Cross Keys. After breakfast make my escape from this large, irregular, busy, opulent, corrupted town; where so many men and so many women use so many ways and means of gaining and spending so much money, and meat, and drink, etc.[1] Set

---
[1] It is to be remembered that at this period of its existence Liverpool was increasing in wealth and importance at an

out for Prescot, a royal borough, and breathe again the air of the country. See on the rising grounds above a fine view of Cheshire and the Welch mountains towards Snowdon and Anglesey. Hay-harvest begun about Prescot; the crop in general but light in this country. At Prescot pass by on my right Knowsly, the seat of Lord Derby. A large pottery-work carried on at Prescot of clay found in its neighbourhood. Betwixt Liverpool and Prescot observed the *Typha latifolia* and the *Jasione*. Betwixt Prescot and Warrington, the road made at the expense of a guinea a yard of *slag*, the refuse of the Copper-works of Warrington and Liverpool, which are now discontinued at both places. This slag is a hard, durable material, and makes the very best road possible. Day becomes sultry upon me in the highest degree.

> 'All-conquering heat, oh, intermit thy wrath!
> And on my throbbing temples potent thus
> Beam not so fierce.'[1]

Stop at Boldheath, and dine. Bowles Hall (an elegant seat of Mrs. Bowles) fronting the room where I dine. Admirably good ale here; said to be the best betwixt Edinburgh and Liverpool; threepence a pint. Pass through Warrington (Squire Bowles Paton on my left as I enter

---

enormous rate, and probably this produced an extravagance which our traveller had not encountered in less commercial communities.

[1] The quotation is from Thomson's *Summer*.

the town).[1] Glass-work here considerable, though no pane-glass made here. Some cotton-looms, but trade dull since the war begun. Warrington streets rather narrow and paltry-looking. Remarkably rich fields and fine cultivation in its neighbourhood. Potatoes, gooseberries, cabbages, etc., in the highest perfection. The ridges are narrow, being about four to six feet broad. The potato preferred here is the *Champion red and white*, and the *American Ranger*. The potatoes here already taken up, and turnips and cabbages (a second crop) in considerable forwardness. New hay in the stack; a great deal in the rick, and most of the hay cut down. Make hay here literally while the sun shines; the girls and hinds following the mowers, with a rake, and constantly tossing and teasing it till it is made. Land here at upwards of five guineas an acre. *Scrophularia aquatica* in the ditches about Warrington. Leave Warrington, and proceed by the Gibbet on my right with a man hung in chains fifty feet high for having robbed the post. Come in sight of the river Irwell (Squire Burnbank's on my right). On my left an extensive tract of moss (Shap[2] Moss). Here is plenty of shell marle used for manure with great success.

In many places here and about Warrington,

[1] Warrington is nearly half-way between Liverpool and Manchester. According to Paterson's *Itinerary*, the distance by road, at that period, was 16½ miles to Liverpool, and 18½ miles to Manchester.
[2] *Read* Chat Moss.

they throw the limestone-shells not slacked into mixtures of rich wet earth from the ditches, etc., layer above layer; the limeshells are thus pulverized by degrees, and the mixture is turned and laid upon the grass sward to very great account. The country far and wide hereabouts is flat, finely enclosed, and well sheltered with wood. As the hedges are high on each side, little is to be seen of the country, save here and there [through] a gap of the hedge, where you have a prospect of a boundless plain country, with farmhouses, strips of wood, rich fields of wheat, beans, potatoes, barley, oats, etc., all waving in the ear. Harvest will begin here in the course of three weeks or so.

About eight miles from Manchester see the *Jasione montana,* and in one place a few plants of *Osmunda regalis* and *Thlaspi campestre.* At the going down of the sun cross the Duke of Bridgewater's canal. Worsley, a seat of His Grace's, on the left on a gentle-rising eminence. Canal runs thirty miles on a level. Curious subterranean works about here. The canal runs underground for miles. The boats go by the light of candles to the very mouths of coal-pits, and are laden under ground. About three miles from Manchester, pass by Bailey's and Simpson's, Esq., magistrates of Manchester. They have elegant country houses here. Evening view of Manchester from the crescent, where the river Irwell takes a beautiful serpentine course, delightful. The country about Manchester has a rich and beautiful aspect. Here again come in sight of *mountains*, without which no landscape can be complete. Come in to Manchester in the evening.

Friday, 10th July. Manchester.—In the morning walk out to see this great manufacturing place; the greatest for all sorts of cotton-works of any in Great Britain. Take a turn to Sir R. Arkwright's great Mills. Thence to the marketplace and centre of the town. Thence in company with a gentleman of the place to the Infirmary and its environs; this by far the prettiest sight about Manchester. The grounds around the Infirmary are elegantly laid out in gardens, gravel-walks, ponds, parterres, etc., where strangers are admitted to walk without any molestation. Adjoining to this place are the Bath-rooms, where ladies and gentlemen are admitted to bathe at one shilling each.

Walk round the Cathedral[1] without and then within; very grand organs; a superb piece of Gothic architecture, having a very neat aspect both without and within. Walk through the different streets and squares of the town;—broader and better-aired than those of Liverpool. The houses many of them four stories high; not crowded as at Liverpool. Much more

---

[1] This is anticipating events. The collegiate church, as it then was, only received cathedral rank in 1848, on the erection of the see of Manchester.

regularity here than at Liverpool. This supposed a larger and more populous place than Liverpool. Population here previous to the commencement of this war estimated at a hundred thousand. It is said to have decreased within these few years upwards of thirty thousand, owing to the recruits for the army and navy, and the emigrants to America.[1]

The place stands by the Cotton-manufacture, which is here carried on through all its stages; and here is the most astonishing display of fancy cotton-stuffs perhaps anywhere to be seen. Immense fortunes have been made in that way here; some individuals to the amount of four hundred thousand pounds sterling. A number of grand churches here; generally with burying-grounds around them. Tomb-stones all flat, and on a level with the surface of the ground, so that they form a fine walk of plain stones. This much the case over the English towns. The inscriptions seem to be by no means diversified. 'Here resteth the body of ——,' with the departure and age of the deceased, inscribed upon almost every one of them; and every one of them a copy of its neighbour. At Liverpool I observed a greater variety in their inscriptions.— College.

Walk over Salford bridge and take a view of

[1] In 1801 the population of Manchester was 75,275, and of Salford, 14,477—together, 89,752. At the census of 1891 the figures were: Manchester, 505,368; Salford, 198,139—together, 703,507.

the old town of Salford, separated from Manchester only by the river Irwell, which is here a dark, nasty stream, polluted by the lees of the manufactures. Return to Manchester, and walk down by the new prison across the river;[1] take to right and view the boats and warehouses on the old black water. From no point have you a good view of Manchester. It is situated in a plain; and the country all round it is a plain.

After dinner, set out by Bridge Street to see the Duke of Bridgewater's canal. Where it terminates (or rather begins) the scene is truly astonishing. It shows what a great spirit with a great fortune may do, and has done. His Grace has laid out his whole fortune upon great public works, which have conduced amazingly to the wealth and convenience and prosperity of this town and country. It is now universally believed that the Duke will be reimbursed and more than reimbursed; he certainly deserves to be so. The dues accruing to him from his canals for the year 1791 were, I was informed, upwards of seventy thousand pounds sterling. He is an old bachelor; a plain, honest man; and affects no pomp or show in his houses, equipage, or mode of living. The world laughed at him for

[1] An antiquarian friend in Manchester writes: 'The reference is to the New Bailey Prison, then only just built, and since demolished. The New Prison was in Salford, so I do not quite follow the diarist: should not "to Manchester" read (or mean) *towards* Manchester?'

undertaking these immense works; he may now laugh at the world in return.

Set out in the cool of the afternoon for Buxton. Keep the London road to Stockport, a large manufacturing town about seven miles south of Manchester: here turn to the left, and after travelling several miles, pass by another gallows with a human body hung in chains, and approach to the hilly country, where have a fine view of Limehall (Colonel Lee) on my right. At the tenth milestone from Buxton, stop and look back north-west towards Manchester and the widely-extended plain, bounded on the north by the Yorkshire mountains, on the east by those of the same county, and of Derbyshire and Cheshire on the east and south-east; towards the west a boundless flat country sloping down as far as the eye can reach towards Liverpool and the Irish Sea. Here leave the flat country and enter the hills.

CHAPTER IV.

Buxton and the Wonders of the Peak.

FRIDAY, 10th July.—Arrive in the evening at Disley, about nine and a half miles from Buxton. Put up all night at the Ram's Head (Hancock), situated in a romantic rural valley; Disley church on a beautiful eminence beside the inn. This place (Disley) lies in Cheshire; the boundary of Derbyshire lies within a few miles on the east. Before supper take a walk up to the church-yard. Walk round the church, which is a pretty model of a country church. The church-yard is planted round with lime trees; and in it there are several good tombstones, with some very tolerable inscriptions.

Saturday, 11th July.—Set out from Disley, and mount the hill. On my right hand long heath enclosed; a group of wild[1] horses somewhat resembling the highlanders, but rather larger in their size, and better shaped. Pass over a

[1] This, of course, only means that the horses were running loose on the moor, as one sees them to-day in the Shetland Islands.

number of hills and dales. Here the limestone is thrown upon the long heath to destroy it and render it fit pasture for sheep. The limestone of Derbyshire is white as chalk. The sheep used here are of the Bakewell kind.

Arrive about one o'clock p.m. at Buxton, and drink the waters before dinner. Considerable number of company here, and more expected when the Parliament rises. This watering-place, however, has not been so much frequented since the war as formerly. Provisions here very high, and living expensive. The Duke of Devonshire, lord of the manor here, has laid out of late years, I am told, more than one hundred and fifty thousand pounds upon buildings here. Fine stone-quarry in the immediate neighbourhood. Vast lime-works. The stables here are supposed to be the most magnificent of any in the kingdom; one hundred and ten fine stalls for horses. The building superb, and admirably executed. Shewn the ladies' and gentlemen's baths. The waters of Buxton always of the same temperature, 82° Fahrenheit; a proof that they rise from a great depth: this circumstance difficult to be accounted for.

Take a walk round the Crescent, the most beautiful building I have anywhere seen. It, with the stables, the work of a great architect, Carr of York. Take a walk in the Great Hall, the most splendid room perhaps in Britain—seventy-five feet long by thirty wide, and thirty-six high. Here the company have balls and assemblies three times every week—Mondays, Wednesdays, and Fridays. Look into the dining-room; also a great room. Here the company dine at three p.m.

After viewing Buxton, walk out to Poole's Hole, about half a mile south in the limestone works. The cave six hundred and ninety yards long. Four old women, resembling the witches of Macbeth, light me into this cave with candles. The cave at present perfectly dry; all but a small spring on the right hand, from which the poor people that live near the entrance take their water, and for which they have to travel every day by candle-light. Petrifactions here very curious, of various forms; lions, organs, beehives, etc. One may walk upright all the way; in some places the roofs are high, and not distinctly to be seen. After viewing this curiosity, the old hags conduct me back by a different track, which again joins the entrance. These poor creatures live in the summer-time almost solely by the gratuities of those gentlemen and ladies who visit the cave; and they sell you also little bits of the different minerals that are to be found in the mountains in this neighbourhood.

Leave Buxton at four p.m., and set out by Tideswell for Castleton in the Peak of Derby. By the way observe the following plants: *Carduus eriophorus, Plantago media, Sanguisorba officinalis, Silene nutans, Centaurea Scabiosa, Anemone Pulsa-*

tilla, Cistus Helianthemum, Geranium sanguineum, etc. The roads and fences all over this country are composed of limestone. Betwixt Tideswell and Castleton, growing plentifully on the refuse of the lime-mines, the *Arenaria saxatilis* (double-flowered). The whole ground covered with lime-kilns.

Arrive at Castleton about eight p.m. Go immediately to see the Devil's ———,[1] supposed to be the greatest thing of the kind in the Island. There is a rope-manufactory at the entrance of the cave; the perpendicular rocks over your head at the entrance are about eighty-seven yards high. The length of the cave is about seven hundred and fifty yards. After proceeding for some time inwards by the light of several candles, you come to water, and are ferried over by your guides in a boat, after which you come into the great hole, seventy yards wide by forty high; its height known. Further on another cave, the height of which is not known.

After getting out of the Devil's ———, conducted about half a mile to the westward, and under a high mountain enter one of the Lead mines (Speedwell). Here at first you descend one hundred and six steps to the boat; then you proceed six hundred and fifty yards in the boat to the Large Cavern, where a cascade bellows like thunder, and finds its way through the

[1] The diarist, of course, gives the older name of the Peak Cavern, which, however, would grate upon the modern ear.

Devil's —— or Peak-hole. The mountain above you is near eight hundred feet; and it is supposed the roof of the cavern may extend to the surface or nearly so, as they have as yet found no top to it; nor indeed any bottom. The cascade falls from the level of the boat fourteen yards perpendicular into a basin about fifty yards in circumference. This basin was plumbed in the centre, and the plummet stuck at the depth of fourteen yards; but it would seem that the rock at this depth slopes away under the mountain to an amazing depth, for the miners informed me that all the rubbish they cut out of this passage for six hundred yards further than the cavern was thrown down into it, and yet it does not fill up in the least. Besides this, there were four boat-loads a day for four years together thrown down into this surprising gulph, each boat at each load carrying four ton weight, and yet it fills none. The boat sails across this unfathomable abyss over an arch thrown across it by the miners; a wonderful work indeed.

The boatmen on our return fixed a burning candle to the rock beside the Cavern, and as we retreated backwards in a straight line from the light, it assumed by degrees the appearance of a star setting in the dark ocean. The tremulous light on the water beyond us, seen at a great distance, produced the finest effect, and had the appearance of tears of light dropping in a perpendicular line from the setting-star. The boatmen entertained us highly all the way to the end of the water, by a charming hunting song, the echo exceeding anything I ever heard.

After leaving the boat, we ascend one hundred and six steps of a stone stair; and gain the open air.—Take my guide with me to the Castleton inn; and arrive there to supper about eleven p.m.

Sunday, 12th July. Castleton in the Peak of Derby.—Went with two guides to Odin Mine, the only Lead-mine worked here at present. About one hundred and twenty hands constantly employed here; have houses at the mouth of the Mine where they reside every day except the Sundays. Here they wash the Lead-ore, and render it fit for the smelting-houses. This Mine goes nearly in a plain about a mile under the hill; the whole is laid with boards, along which the miners drag out the lead-ore on four-wheeled carriages to the houses at the entrance.

In walking along the foot of the hill towards this Mine, the traveller is struck with the appearance of the limestone-fences that enclose the grounds here-abouts. Each stone is a congeries of the most curious petrifactions of shells, pectens, worms, and other bodies seemingly of marine production. The stone-fences betwixt Tideswell and Castleton are distinguished by the same phenomena; difficult to be accounted for by the naturalist.

From Odin Mine we ascended the hill, till we came to the mouth of the Mine, where the Blue

John (*Fluor spatosus*) is found. The miners here say that it is found nowhere else in the world. This is a very curious spar of different beautiful colours; curiously wrought into different kinds of utensils, and sold at a very high price; great demand for it from different places of the world. Discovered about thirty or forty years ago by the [? late] Mr. Hall of this country.

Here having got dressed as a miner, I descended after my two guides into the bowels of the mountain for hundreds of yards through narrow, difficult and dangerous passages, sometimes crawling, sometimes stooping, sometimes standing, sometimes sliding through wet clay and red ochre, till we came at last to the bottom of one of the most beautiful Caverns in nature. Here having missed one of my guides, I began to enquire about him of the other, who, without giving me any direct answer, desired me to step down a little further. When we had got down a few steps—'Look up now,' says he. I looked up to my utter astonishment indeed! into a cavern upwards of one hundred feet high above us completely illuminated as a drawing-room, a lustre of six candles suspended from a rock that jutted into the cavity about seventy feet over my head, the light wonderfully reflected from all sides of the Cavern by a thousand different kinds of spars, icicles, incrustations and petrifactions, resembling birds, beasts, fishes, serpents, and different creatures and different objects, glittering all round from the bottom up the cavity as far as the eye and the light could penetrate. On observing the lustre above I found it was supported by the hand of the other guide, who had ingeniously withdrawn himself on purpose to surprise us; he was standing on a pinnacle of the rock where I could not conceive it possible for a human being to stand; and therefore his appearance struck me at first with the idea of some supernatural being, inhabiting a region of enchantment. My guide from below hollowed up to him; the voice resounded through the superior regions of the Cavern; and the guide from above immediately struck up a solemn church-tune, the notes of which reverberated from the rocks and caves around, exciting in my mind sentiments of the most awful devotion. The choir of the most magnificent cathedral could not produce a more powerful effect upon the mind.

After having been conducted to the place where the Blue John is found, and shewn very distinctly the disposition of its strata and the manner of working it, we ascended from this region of subterraneous wonders to the light of day; and, having refreshed ourselves with a glass of rum and a crust of bread, we then directed our course to Elden-hole, upon the high grounds about three miles southwest of Castleton. This is a tremendous Gap about thirty yards long and in some places not exceeding two yards broad; its depth has never yet been fathomed; the upper regions of it seem to be inhabited principally by Jack-daws. We threw down six large stones, and listened for several seconds to the sound of each. One or two of them were interrupted in their descent; the rest were heard at an amazing distance, and one or two seemed to emit a sound as if they fell into water. Here I was entertained by my guide with many wonderful stories with respect to this hole; some of which are authenticated beyond any doubt. It is very properly enclosed with a high stone-wall, to prevent danger.—Return to Castleton, where stay all night.

Monday, 13th July.—Rise in the morning, and before breakfast ascend the hill to the south of the town, to view the ruins of the Castle. It stands directly above the Peak-hole, the foundation of the Castle eighty-seven yards perpendicular above the entrance into that awful Cavern. This has been a very strong building; and it is so old as to be beyond the reach of written record or even oral tradition.[1] The *Allium vincale* is said to grow here, but I saw it not.

After breakfast leave Castleton, and set out for Sheffield through the country of the Peak, lying romantic and retired along the banks of the Derwent, the mountains forming a *cul-de-sac* upon the west. Here observe by the way-side great plenty of *Betonica officinalis, Geranium pratense,*

---

[1] Had *Peveril of the Peak* been then written, the diarist would have known that this was Peveril Castle, built by a son of William the Conqueror.

Genista tinctoria, etc. After leaving the Peak, ascend a steep hill, and look back towards Castleton; the road here rises by a long winding ascent to a very considerable elevation. Pass along the level of the high grounds, excluded for some time from the sight of any human abode. Here fall in with a shepherd regaling on his simple fare, his flocks feeding around him on the short heathy hill. It was two p.m., and the day was hot and sultry. The sight of this simple swain, in his pastoral solitude, recalled to my mind the following beautiful pastoral of Cunningham, which I amused myself by repeating aloud as I journeyed along the hill:

'O'er moorlands and mountains, rude, barren and bare,
As wilder'd and wearied I roam,' etc.[1]

From this reverie, however, I was soon awakened by the sudden bursting in upon my sight of one of the most extensive and striking prospects I have ever contemplated. From an elevation of many hundred feet high the town of Sheffield appears at your feet, with the charming country around it; on your right hand the level part of Derbyshire; and before you, towards the north and north-east, the rich Ridings of Yorkshire are seen stretching out in boundless extent to where they are lost in the verge of the horizon.

Come down to Sharrow-head about three o'clock

[1] The opening lines of 'Content : A Pastoral,' by John Cunningham, Irish poet and dramatist (1729-1773).

p.m. Find my good old friend Mr. Mackenzie[1] at home. We have not seen one another for ten years. The meeting such as might be expected, but cannot well be described. The world has made him fortunate, but it has not made him proud, nor changed his nature in the smallest degree. The same independence of sentiment, the same benevolence of disposition, the same generosity of heart, not to be impaired by time, place, or circumstances. He receives me with all that warmth of affection, and with all those delicate attentions, by which true friendship can at any time be distinguished.

Here I and my horse rest, and are thankful!

[1] The Rev. Alexander Mackenzie, curate of St. Paul's, Sheffield, from 1789 to 1816, and previously chaplain to the Earl of Eglinton. A beautiful monument by Chantrey was erected to his memory in the church of which he was incumbent. It appears that he acquired the estate of Sharrowhead by his marriage with the niece of the former proprietor, a Mr. Batty. He is described as 'one of the six men in the town who were above 6 feet high,' and at the date of the Diary he was forty-one years of age. It may be added that the references to his personal character made by others quite justify the warm admiration bestowed upon him by his friend the diarist. (See Dr. Gatty's edition of Hunter's *Hallamshire*, 1869, p. 275; and Mr. R. E. Leader's *Reminiscences of Old Sheffield*, 1876, p. 103.)

CHAPTER V.

Sheffield—In the Stage-Coach to London *viâ* Nottingham, Leicester and Northampton.

MONDAY, 13th July.—Take an evening walk with my friend to Sheffield, and view the town. Find there our countrymen, Captain McDonald, Dalchoshnie,[1] Captain Alexander Stewart of Balnakeilly, and a Captain McKilligan of Banff; the two last officers of the Sheffield Regiment. Go to the new Infirmary and Barracks.

Tuesday, 14th July. Sharrow-head.—In the morning at breakfast have the pleasure of blessing the three lovely children of my friend. They had been the day before out on a visit, and I have

[1] That is, of the family of McDonald of Dalchoshnie, or Dalchosnie, Perthshire. This officer may have been Alexander, the son and heir of the then laird, or he may have been a younger son, Donald, who afterwards distinguished himself at Waterloo, where he commanded the 92nd Highlanders. The Dalchoshnie family has a brilliant military record. The father and grandfather of this officer fought in the Jacobite army of 1745-46, and of five brothers in the fourth generation *all* were in the army. (See Burke's *Landed Gentry*.)

not seen them till now. To see those whom we love, and to see them prosperous, happy, and respected, affords to an ingenuous mind a satisfaction not to be expressed!

Go down with my friend to Sheffield, and dine at the Tontine[1] with our countrymen the two captains (having first in the forenoon taken a turn with Mr. Mackenzie to see the Snuff-mills of this place, on a wonderful scale by the Messrs. Wilson).

Wednesday, 15th July.—Walk down to the Tontine, and call upon our friends the two captains, who accompany us to Sharrow-head to dinner. After dinner go down to the parade, and have a view of the Sheffield Regiment. Return in the evening to the hospitable house of my friend, and converse with him *tête-à-tête*, at and after supper, on 'the days of former years.'[2]

Thursday, 16th July.—Take a ride out with my friend to Norton in Derbyshire, and dine there

---

[1] This was one of the many 'Tontine' inns, so called because the money for their erection was subscribed on the 'tontine' system. The Tontine at Sheffield, which was completed in 1785, appears to have been one of the best inns of the day. 'Dr. Gatty gives a good description of what it was in its glory, when "twenty horses and five postboys were always ready when the yard-bell rang," and how suddenly it collapsed on the opening of the Midland Railway. . . . "Thus one of the fine old English inns, in the courtyard of which a carriage and pair could be easily driven round, came to grief."' (See Dr. Gatty's edition of Hunter's *Hallamshire*, 1869, p. 199 ; and R. E. Leader's *Reminiscences of Old Sheffield*, 1876, pp. 214, 215.)

[2] This quotation reminds one that Macpherson's *Ossian* was at that time very much in the air.

with the Norton Club, a very agreeable society of gentlemen who meet there once a week, and of which society my friend is a member both beloved and esteemed, as he is by every society who know him. Here we have an elegant rural repast, and play in the afternoon at bowls on a beautiful bowling-green on a high, healthy situation adjoining to the inn, where we dined with Mr. Smith, brother-in-law to my friend, a pleasant gentleman possessed of a considerable fortune already, and having a much greater one in prospect. The other gentlemen this day at the club were a Mr. Staniforth, a merchant in Sheffield, and a Mr. Parker, a gentleman of the law there.

Returning in the evening to Sharrow, as we descended the hill from Norton towards the bank of the Sheff [or Sheaf], which here separates the County of York from that of Derby, we enjoy one of the first of prospects. The town of Sheffield lies in the heart of finely swelling hills that rise all round it, adorned with well-cultivated fields, beautiful plantations, and enclosures, with a vast number of elegant seats of gentlemen, all enjoying the finest situation.

Have another agreeable *tête-à-tête* with my friend after supper. Go to bed and enjoy sweet repose.

Friday, 17th July. Sharrow.—Go down in the forenoon to Sheffield with my friend, and call upon the two captains, etc. Thence am conducted to see the Steam-engines, the Cutlery-works, the Coalerie of the Duke of Norfolk; with which highly gratified.

Mr. Mackenzie conducts me to the shop of a cutler, where I purchase, strange to tell! twelve good knives with cases at the rate of one shilling, and have my own penknife sharpened into the bargain. To one who has not seen the amazing works of this place, such a circumstance appears truly incredible. These knives are here made in vast quantities at this low rate, and sent over to Germany. Amazing fortunes rapidly made here by cutlery-works; and people rising every day from nothing to eminence, by dint of industry. This day have also a view of the great ironworks, and the method of refining iron in the furnace and under the hammer. This an astonishing work; a semblance to Carron.[1]

Return at two p.m. to Sharrow. Dress, and go with my friend to dine at the elegant country-seat of Mr. William Shore,[2] a man whose grandfather was a common hammerman, and who now enjoys a fortune of some thousands a year. I was a good deal struck with the elegance and luxury of his table. A numerous company of ladies and gentlemen, viz., Misses Walker from Manchester, Miss Hutchinson of Sheffield, Mr. Grieve, Mr. Wyat,

[1] The famous ironworks of Carron, in Stirlingshire, were established by Dr. Roebuck, of Sheffield, in 1760. It was here that 'carronades' were first made, whence their name.

[2] This was evidently Mr. William Shore, of Tapton Hill. A son of his, who assumed his maternal uncle's name of Nightingale, was the father of Miss Florence Nightingale. (See Dr. Gatty's *Sheffield: Past and Present*, 1873, p. 177.)

etc., equally pleasant in their persons and in their manners. Mr. Shore takes me to see his place and garden: his is one of the first seats in this neighbourhood. Stay here till after supper, and walk home with my friend to Sharrow, highly pleased with the manner in which we have spent the day.

Saturday, 18th July. Sharrow.—Walk down to Sheffield, and call upon the two captains. Come up with them to Sharrow to dinner. Company at dinner this day in the house of my friend consists of the worthy Landlord himself, Mr. Jo: Walker, a very rich man; Mr. Smith, brother-in-law to Mr. Mackenzie, Mr. Grieve, Captain Alexander Stewart, and Captain McKilligan, Mr. Lamprier, Mr. Wilson, Mr. Preston,[1] the parson of Sheffield, Mr. Elliot.

A hearty and happy company as ever I sat in; and entertained by my worthy friend in the most easy and elegant style of hospitality. After tea a party at whist; and a number of the company stay supper.

Sunday, 19th July. Sharrow.—This day accompany Mr. Mackenzie to Dronfield, about five miles from Sharrow. He here introduces me to the amiable family of his brother-in-law, Mr. Smith. Mrs. Smith, his mother, an old, infirm, sensible woman. Young Mrs. Smith, a pleasant, elegant woman, extremely affable and attentive to strangers.

[1] The Rev. Matthew Preston, 'assistant-minister of Sheffield' from 1776 to 1829.

Go to the church of Dronfield with Mrs. Smith, younger, and a Miss Holwell, a daughter of a clergyman in Devonshire. Have an elegant and affecting sermon from Mr. Mackenzie. The choir here somewhat singular. After sermon return to Mr. Smith's house, and see his garden, his dogs, and his horses. This gentleman has a good fortune, and the prospect of a very considerable addition to it; amiable, mild, and complaisant in his manners. Dine here with the family, and introduced to a Mrs. ——, a Scotch lady.

After dinner return to the church in the afternoon, and hear another very affecting discourse from my friend. He is a very popular man in this country, and deserves to be so in the best sense of the word. The Service for the recovery of a woman after childbirth. Hear a curious chorus perform an Anthem in vocal and instrumental music, flutes, hautboys, etc. It has a very pleasing effect upon me, unaccustomed to such exhibitions. The audience extremely attentive to my friend, and seemingly much affected by his sermon. After sermon the bells ring all the afternoon in honour of my friend. He here performs the funeral service over the corpse of a child. Mr. Smith and I accompany him to witness it. After which return to tea. After tea walk out with the company, and view the village and its very romantic neighbourhood. Take leave of our friends in the evening, and ride home by the bridle-way to Sharrow.

Monday, 20th July. Sharrow.—Leave my horse with my friend. Set out at half-past three o'clock a.m. with Mr. Mackenzie's boy carrying my saddle-bags to the Toll-bar separating the counties of York and Derby, where take my seat on the stage-coach at half-past four. Breakfast at Chesterfield, remarkable for its twisted spire, apparently crooked, and like to fall. Mr. Wilkinson, the banker, has an elegant house on the east side of the town.

Mount our coach after swallowing breakfast in a few minutes, and set out again in company of a Mr. Mackenzie[1] from Sheffield. Stevens, a blind man, entertains us highly all the way, with music on a fife and a fiddle, and sings like a nightingale. The weather exceedingly warm and favourable, enjoy a delightful view of the country from the outside of the coach. Arrive about ten a.m. at Mansfield, where our jolly blind piper leaves us. Set out for Nottingham, along Sherwood Forest, fourteen miles long. Some fine old trees scattered here and there over it; some places of it begin to be well cultivated. Dine at Nottingham, a large and elegant town, finely situated on the north bank of the Trent, a broad river here (with a bridge of seventeen arches), which has its course to north-east, and at last joins the Humber. The streets, houses, and

---

[1] Perhaps a slip of the diarist's or of the transliterator's: it seems unlikely that this surname should be so common in Sheffield at that time.

market-place here broad, cleanly, and elegant. The castle stands on a high rock at the west end of the town. A remarkable bed shewn here of Queen Anne.

After leaving Nottingham, pass the bridge, and for some miles look back on one of the most charming prospects in England. Come in the afternoon to Loughborough; the streets here rather narrow, dirty, and irregular. From hence proceed to Leicester, where arrive about six p.m. This also a spacious and elegant town. The old tapestry-work revived here by an ingenious lady. After running a little through the streets and market-place, to get a cursory view of it, drink tea with two ladies from Mansfield; two young boys, a gentleman of fortune's sons in the neighbourhood of Nottingham, with their tutor, Monsr. Egrace, a French priest; and a Mr. Coleman of Leicester, a sea-faring gentleman, who accompany us all the way to London.

From Leicester to Harborough. From thence by star-light to Northampton, where we arrive about three o'clock a.m. on the morning of Tuesday. This one of the first market-places, with the best houses and streets of any town in England. Leave Northampton, and proceed to Newport-Pagnell to breakfast. From thence to Wooburne [Woburn] in Bedfordshire. Have a fine view of the Duke of Bedford's. His deer-park fourteen miles round: many fallow and some red deer here. House to be seen only on

Mondays. His Grace supposed to be the richest duke in England.

Arrive at Dunstable, where enter Hartfordshire. From Dunstable set out for St. Albans, and pass on three miles beyond it to a good inn, where dine. After dinner set out for Barnet. Haymakers on every hand busy; a fine crop appearing everywhere. Here take the outside of the coach to view the country. Dreadful thunderstorm. At Highgate have a view of the Thames, the City, etc., etc.

'Heav'ns! what a goodly prospect spreads around!'

Enter the Capital by Islington, and arrive at half-past five p.m. at the Bull-and-Mouth Inn near Aldersgate, where put up all night, and enjoy comfortable repose, having had none for the two preceding nights, and having in the course of thirty-six hours travelled one hundred and sixty-five miles.

CHAPTER VI.

London and Windsor.

*W*EDNESDAY, 22nd July. London.—Rise at eight o'clock a.m. and dress. After breakfast, write a letter to my friend Captain Patrick Mackenzie of the Royals, Corsica. In the forenoon it rains hard. Not choosing to venture abroad to deliver my letters, I amuse myself in the house, by extending my Notes, and perusing the London Directory, &c.

Dine at the Bull-and-Mouth Inn. Walk out in the afternoon to St. Paul's Churchyard. Walk round St. Paul's Church, and take a general view of that stately monument. Though by all accounts the second in Europe, it wants uniformity in its external appearance, not being equally balanced on each side of the cupola. Sir Christopher Wren intended something else than what has been executed in his name.—From St. Paul's Churchyard direct my course to Blackfriars Bridge. From thence have a grand view of the town, the river, and the shipping down by London Bridge;

and of Temple Gardens, Somerset House, the Adelphi, &c., up the river.

Pass Blackfriars Bridge, and set out along the south side of the river to Westminster Bridge. Arrive there happily in time to witness a grand anniversary sailing match on the river. The prize a silver bowl, run for by six barges with four men in each; the distance from Blackfriars Bridge to Putney Bridge, about eight miles up the river, and back again to opposite Vauxhall. The vast concourse of people on the Bridge and on each side of the river, the vast number of boats and barges with splendid company on board, the rowers keeping time in the most regular harmony, &c., was to me a scene of perfect astonishment. While engaged in the contemplation of this scene, whom do I observe on the bridge beside me but my old school and college-fellow Mr. David Ritchie, depute-chaplain to the Scotch Brigade. Tap him on the shoulder; he turns about and immediately recognises me. We walk together arm-in-arm up the river on the Westminster side to view the boats on their return from Putney; each bank of the river lined with a crowd of spectators almost impenetrable. Take our station opposite to Vauxhall. About half-past seven the boats return with the returning tide, preceded by a very unusual and extraordinary spectacle; viz.:—A most magnificent barge, constructed somewhat in the form of Neptune's triumphal car, as described by Virgil and the old Roman and Grecian poets.

This elegant, expensive, fanciful machine, it seems, was first designed in honour of Lord Howe's Victory over the French fleet;[1] and it has lately been altered a little in honour of the Prince of Wales' marriage.[2] It was accompanied by a thousand other barges with ladies and gentlemen; and as it dropt slow down the river, its wheels seemed to move upon the surface of the water, and it appeared to be drawn along by two large sea-monsters having the necks and manes and heads of horses that proudly arched their necks, and moved their heads, and bit their reins as they moved along the deep. In the Car aloft the torch of Hymen burned, while Cupids fanned the flame. In the mean time the musical band of the Duke of York, that is, the Band of the Horse Guards, being stationed on board this wonderful machine, performed the most sublime pieces of music in the most masterly manner; the notes coming softened along the water, produced on all sides the most admirable effects.

Soon after this watery procession had stopped past the Park Bridge, the sailing-racers came down the river with vast rapidity, accompanied also by a thousand barges covering the whole surface of the Thames. While the gaining vessel approached to the goal, the guns were fired on

---

[1] Off Ushant, June 1, 1794.
[2] George IV., at that time Prince of Wales, was married to Princess Caroline of Brunswick on April 8, 1795.

each side : and the whole vessels in the evening sailed down towards Westminster Bridge, while the crowds on each side of the river withdrew by slow degrees to the City. Even in the most luxurious times of ancient Rome, never sure could old Father Tiber boast a nobler spectacle.

Mr. Ritchie and I retire immediately to his apartment in Barton Street, Westminster, where we drink tea in the company of a French priest. After tea, we walk up together along the side of the river again. Take a boat and sail over to Vauxhall by the light of the moon. The evening being very favourable, this was by far the grandest exhibition at Vauxhall this season. The company very numerous and brilliant. Much struck with the illuminations, walks, arbours, &c.; but more with the appearance of the company; and more still with their manners. Evening-singing in the Orchestra ; songs by Mrs. Mountain, Mr. Taylor, &c. The Vauxhall band and the Duke of York's play by turn.

About eleven p.m. my friend Ritchie and I retire to a box and refresh ourselves with a bottle of Port. Various reflections arise in our minds during the different stages of the entertainment. Curious attachments formed here. Vast numbers of ladies of pleasure. The manners of most of these seem rather calculated to confirm virtue than to weaken its influence on the reflecting mind. Good heavens! what prostitution and corruption prevail in this City ! What a contrast this to the Lakes of Cumberland,[1] and the Caves of Yorkshire, &c.! Do not many of these strumpets seem modest? and are not many of them even of an angelic form? But alas! it is plainly nothing else but outward semblance; within all is vice and rottenness! Corrupted themselves, they make it their business to corrupt the heedless and the unwary. And these beautiful young creatures, these female *children*, what have they to do here at this time of the night, or rather of the morning, when they ought to sleep in their beds at home? 'Alas!' said my friend, 'they are drawn into these haunts of vice by women who are old in vice themselves and who glory in training up these poor infants in the ways of wickedness.' It is now two in the morning, and the scene begins to be riot and dissipation. 'Let us withdraw for a little,' says he, 'into this dark and solitary arbour.' 'Seest thou yon stars, my friend, that twinkle over our heads in the azure heavens?' 'Ay,' says Ritchie, 'the smallest of them is greater than the globe of this Earth.' 'Then,' said I, 'how exceedingly contemptible are the lights of Vauxhall, and how soon are they extinguished!— Enough of it. I am satisfied. Let us quit this scene; and betake ourselves to our respective homes.'[2]

[1] Visited by the diarist in 1794.
[2] Although the moralisings of these two worthy parsons contain nothing very striking in themselves, they help to complete this picture of a night at Vauxhall Gardens, towards the close of the eighteenth century.

We walk together to Westminster Bridge, and bid good-night. Three a.m. struck solemnly from St. Paul's, as I mused alone through the Churchyard. A watchman conducts me to my lodgings.

Thursday, 23rd July. London.—About ten o'clock a.m., walk to Blackfriars Bridge on purpose to take a boat up the river to Westminster, but find it impracticable on account of the high west wind and the want of the tide. Saunter on foot along the Strand to Covent Garden, where enquire in different places for Forbes the bookseller, but could not possibly find him. Proceed to Westminster. Call upon Mr. Humphrey Donaldson, Army-Agent, Whitehall, and have the happiness of finding him in his Counting-room. Front view of the Horse Guards. Proceed by the Parliament House to Fludyers Street, and deliver my letters to Captain Mackay. Thence by Westminster College to Barton Street, to the lodgings of Mr. Ritchie, who accompanies me to Westminster Abbey. Walk round this stupendous place, and take a view of the Monuments. Thence to James's Park. View of Charleton [Carlton] House, St. James', Buckingham Palace, house of Mr. Pitt, &c.

Dine at four p.m. at the Golden Cross Hotel. Thence proceed to Oxford Street, to the house of my friend Mr. John Brodie, baker, who insists upon my staying in his house as his guest till I leave London. Walk with him after tea to

Holborn, and away to the Bull-and-Mouth Inn, near Aldersgate, where I clear my bill, call a coach, put my saddle-bags, Mr. Brodie and myself on board, and drive to Mr. Brodie's, where arrive about eight in the evening. Mr. Brodie accompanies me through a number of the streets and squares of Mary-le-bone. This a Parish of vast extent, lying to the north of Oxford Street: the buildings all of the most magnificent sort. Residence this of vast numbers of the gentry and nobility of the two kingdoms. Elegance and conveniency joined to magnificence; superior to anything I have yet seen; and containing more inhabitants, this parish alone, it is said, than all Edinburgh put together. After walking through many of the squares and streets of this wonderful place, Mary-le-bone, my friend Mr. Brodie and I arrive fatigued at his house about ten. Sup, and go to bed.

Friday, 24th July. London.—After breakfast set out by the Haymarket to Charing Cross. Thence to James's Park. The Horse Guards march from the King's Palace along the Park to the Parade, an admirable Band of music playing all the way. Go down along with them to see them drawn up, near the house of Mr. Pitt. At half-past eleven a.m. step into a coach, and set out for Blackheath along Westminster Bridge. Pass through a part of the Counties of Surrey and Kent. Come to Deptford, separated from Greenwich by a small brook. Arrive at Blackheath about one p.m. Surprise my old friend Mr. Fisher of the Academy there. Find him comfortably situated with an amiable wife and five sweet children. This a pleasing sight to me, and a sight too that conveys a serious lesson of morality to me. Introduced here to a Count Duroure, a French gentleman of the Army, one of the many French refugees now in Great Britain.[1] Messrs. Ritchie and Gibson arrive at Blackheath to dinner. After dinner go in the afternoon to see Greenwich Hospital, the first piece of architecture in Britain; a striking proof of the munificent spirit of its Royal Founders and of the generosity and opulence of the British Nation. As we approach to it from Greenwich Park by the Observatory, the grandeur of the Hospital itself, with the beautifully diversified grounds in its vicinity; the river Thames and the Shipping, for many miles winding in a serpentine direction up to London; the numerous spires of the City seen distinct and at different distances through the trees; the finely-cultivated grounds of Middlesex and Essex on the other side of the river before us; with the suburbs of

[1] This was perhaps the Count Duroure who made himself somewhat conspicuous in London in the latter part of 1784 (see the *Annual Register* for that year, pp. 90, 96, 97, and 103, of 'Principal Occurrences'). At that date he was about 28 years of age,' and was described as 'Lieutenant Duroure, late of the horse-guards Blue,' and as 'of a noble family in France.' It is to be noted, however, that his father was then alive and in the service of the King of France. Consequently, the *émigré* of the Diary may have been the father, not the son.

London stretching out in boundless extent, and the rising-grounds about Highgate and Hampstead in the back part of the scene; form altogether such a prospect as is not to be described, and I believe is seldom to be seen upon the surface of this Globe.

Having surveyed at leisure the Council Chamber, the Painted Hall, the bold design and masterly execution of Sir James Thornhill, together with the other departments of this magnificent Structure (one thousand four hundred Pensioners dine in one Hall); we took our leave of Mr. Fisher and the Count, and set out again for the Metropolis in a long-coach,[1] and in the company of twenty ladies and gentlemen, disposed in two rows, facing each other, and moving laterally, in this manner forming an agreeable party; and joking and conversing together on different subjects, we arrived about half-past nine at Charing Cross, where, on account of the heavy rain, we were taken up in different coaches according to our different distances; Mr. Gibson and I setting out together for Oxford Street, where arrive in due time to supper.

Saturday, 25th July. London.—Get up at five a.m., and go with Mr. Brodie to see the Green-market at Covent Garden. This an unusual and very astonishing scene; perhaps the first green-

[1] The ordinary covered stage-coach was then known as a 'short coach,' while a 'long coach' was probably an open brake. (See Mrs. Grant's *Letters from the Mountains*, vol. iii., Letter XLI.)

market of any in the world; and three times crowded every week, Saturday being the principal day. There are several other green-markets in London; but this by far the greatest. It is impossible to form any idea of the vast profusion of roots, and herbs, and flowers, and fruits, of all sorts and of the very best qualities, all in perfect maturity, packed up in the most cleanly, secure, and ingenious manner, in hampers, and barrows, and baskets, and carts, and waggons, &c.; and here and there green-houses, with varieties of green-house plants for sale; with thousands rushing in from every quarter, and women (principally Welch and Irish) walking with immense loads of fruits, &c., on their heads from the distance of perhaps six or eight miles or more from Kent, and Surrey, and Middlesex, and Essex, &c. Nothing to be seen here for many hours of the morning, but bustle and hurry, cooks and cook-maids, scullions and kitchen-boys, men-servants and maid-servants, and people of every denomination and description, carrying off from this great market vegetable-luxuries of every kind, to satisfy the luxurious appetites of this immense Metropolis; so that almost before noon-day every thing is disposed of, and the bustle ceases.

In the forenoon went with Miss Mary and Miss Nancy Brodie to see the Panorama. Spent two hours with great pleasure contemplating and admiring this wonderful power of perspective.

In one apartment is exhibited a most striking view of Lord Howe's Victory of the First June, 1794. In another department the City of London, viewed from the Albion Mills; sixty-five Spires.—Before dinner, went with Mr. Brodie and Mr. Gray to see the Porter Brewery of Mr. Meux. His largest Vat twice the size of that of Mr. Whitbread; twenty-five feet high; one hundred and ninety-five feet in circumference; and contains twenty thousand Barrels. His second Vat half this size. Taste of his Porter drawn off from this second vat. Mr. Meux is extending his scale of operations, and is determined to be the first Porter Brewer in London, that is, in the world.

In the afternoon Mr. Brodie accompanies me to Chelsea Hospital up the Thames some miles from London. After taking an outside prospect of the buildings, went in to see the wards. The old soldiers here on a very comfortable footing; as the old sailors are at Greenwich. Amazing cleanliness and order preserved in the Hospital. Take a view of the Hall, where one hundred and fifty of the Pensioners dine together. Here Charles II. is portrayed on a very large scale, with several striking emblematical figures around him. From the Great Hall went into the Chapel. Here is a very fine painting of our Saviour's Ascension, the work of the celebrated Sebastian Ricci.—From Chelsea walk up Sloane's Street, and away to Kensington. Here fall in accidentally with Mr.

Forsyth of the King's Gardens,[1] who treats us with great kindness and attention. Walk home in the evening through Hyde Park, where see some of the finest women I ever saw in my life. Arrive at Oxford Street to supper.

Sunday, 26th July. Windsor.—Rise and set out by New Bond Street to Piccadilly, where take the coach at half-past six a.m., and passing through Kensington, Turnam-green, Hammersmith, Brentford, Hounslow, Maidenhead, &c., arrive about eleven a.m. at Eton and Windsor, which are separated from one another by the Thames. View of Eton College. Breakfast at the White Hart, Windsor. After breakfast go to St. George's Chapel, one of the finest churches in the world. Remark the painted windows and altar-piece. Hear divine service performed here. The Organs remarkably soft and melodious. See the King and Queen, the Princess Royal, and three other of the young Princes, together with the Duchess of York, and the Prince of Orange, &c. After divine service the King and Queen with the Duchess of York go up to the Palace in one coach, the Princes in another, the Princess Royal and the Prince of Orange, with some of the Ladies in Waiting, walking up to the Palace, the day being exceedingly fine.

Walk for an hour through Windsor forest.

[1] William Forsyth, F.L.S. Born at Old Meldrum, Aberdeenshire, in 1737. Appointed Superintendent of the Royal Gardens at Kensington in 1784. Died in 1804. (See Chambers' *Biographical Dictionary*.)

Then up to the Terrace, where enjoy one of the finest inland prospects that can anywhere be seen. Join the company to see the Paintings in the Castle. Windsor a favourite residence of His Majesty, and no wonder; it is by far the first palace he has. From the Round Tower one can see very distinctly on a clear day the Cupola of St. Paul's, and several spires of the city of London. The country finely wooded and well cultivated round Windsor; and the Thames is seen winding most sweetly along by Eton, and hiding his head in the majestic shades of Windsor.

' Ye distant spires, ye antique tow'rs
That crown the wat'ry glade,' etc.

Mount the stage-coach again at 4 p.m., and enjoy a delightful evening ride to London. Observe by the wayside from my airy vehicle great plenty of the *Sagittaria sagittifolia*, the *Butomus umbellatus*, &c. About the walls of Windsor Castle plenty of *Asplenium Ruta muraria, Antirrhinum Cymbalaria*, &c. Arrive at Hyde Park Corner in the evening. St. James's Park and Hyde Park crowded with company walking. Elegant show of beauty and fashion.

Monday, 27th July. London.—Set out in the morning in a coach by Holborn, the Mansion House, the Bank of England, &c., to Billingsgate. This a curious scene. Here swallow a fresh haddock nicely dressed, and drink a pot of porter with Messrs. Brodie and Webster, with whom take a boat and sail down the Thames through the shipping to within a very few miles of Gravesend.

Pleasant company on board the *Blossom*. Delightful view of the coasts of Kent and Essex. Come in prospect of the East India Fleet just arrived in the river; six millions of pounds sterling. Get along-side of the *Phœnix*, East Indiaman. Pleasant and affecting interview with Mr. George Brodie of that ship. Get immediately on board. Dine there. See on board an Elephant, a present from the Nabob of Arcot to Her Majesty the Queen of Britain. See there also a curious monkey, some Java sparrows, an elk, and several sheep of the Cape of Good Hope, &c., &c.

Great luxury and elegance on board the East India ships. Take leave of our friends here, and sail up in an open boat to Wapping by the light of the moon. Get on shore at Wapping by ten p.m. Walk up from Wapping by Tower Hill, &c., &c., to Oxford Street, nearly six miles. Arrive safe at home by half-past eleven, p.m. Sleep soundly after the numerous and striking adventures of the day.

Tuesday, 28th July. London.—Go in the forenoon with Misses Margaret and Nancy Brodie to visit St. Paul's. This one of the most superb edifices in the world. See the model of it as originally intended by Sir Christopher Wren. Height of the Dome of St. Paul's four hundred and four feet above the pavement. Length of

St. Paul's from east to west within the walls, five hundred and ten feet. From north to south within the doors of the porticos, two hundred and eighty-two feet. Its circuit two thousand two hundred and ninety-two feet. Extent of the ground-plat whereon St. Paul's stands, two acres, sixteen perches, twenty-three yards, one foot.

The Library very curious. Some strange antique manuscripts shown here. Whispering Gallery very amazing. The smallest whisper heard here one hundred and forty feet distant from the whisperer in a straight line. This effect produced by the rotundity of the Dome. Shutting of the doors of the Dome like thunder. Ascend with the ladies from the whispering-gallery all the way to the golden gallery, and from thence to the top of the Cupola. Go out and walk round here. It blowing a fresh gale, and the smoke of the city being thereby cleared away, have a very stupendous view of London, the river, the bridges, the shipping, &c., perhaps the *richest* prospect in the world.—Descend to the pavement within, by upwards of six hundred steps. Take a view of the organs, the inside of the Cathedral where divine service is performed, the Altar, &c.: and return to Oxford Street, after having been five hours absent from it.

In the afternoon walk out through the parks to the north of Mary-le-bone, and ascend the rising grounds at Hampstead. The prospect of London, &c., from this elevation is very pleasant; and this is the point from which Thomson is supposed to begin the description that introduces his admirable panegyric upon Great Britain :

> 'Heav'ns ! what a goodly prospect spreads around,
> Of hills, and dales, and woods, and lawns, and spires,
> And glitt'ring towns, and gilded streams,' etc.

Wednesday, 29th July. London.—Go down after breakfast by New Bond Street, where meet by accident my friend Mr. Josiah Walker from Eton, who informs me that the Marquis of Tullibardine had that morning sailed for the Continent on his travels.[1]

Call upon my old pupils Misses Euphemia and Maria French in Dover Street. This a very unexpected and pleasing interview.—Walk thence to the Court of St. James's Palace, and see the shifting of the Guards. The Duke of York's Band, and the Duke of Gloucester's; both remarkably fine. Great concourse of people here to witness this sight.—Saunter down through St. James' Park to Westminster Abbey.—Walk in and view again the tombs. Proceed afterwards by Westminster College to the lodgings of Mr. Ritchie. Not finding him within, take a coach and go out alone to Greenwich. Walk up through Greenwich Park by the Observatory,

---

[1] This Marquis of Tullibardine was the eldest son of John, fourth Duke of Atholl, whom he succeeded in 1830. In explanation of his interest in the movements of the young Marquis, it may be stated that a portion of the Atholl estates lies in the diarist's parish, and that the Dukes of Atholl were (conjointly with the Earls of Airlie) patrons of his living.

and arrive at my friend Mr. Fisher's to dinner. After dinner Mr. and Mrs. Fisher, Mr. Ritchie, Count Duroure and I walk out to see the ruins of Sir Gregory Page's house in the Park adjoining. This has been one of the finest houses in England: and the grounds and trees about it disposed in the finest manner.[1] Spend the evening at Blackheath, and pass the night with my friend.

Thursday, 30th July. London.—Leave Blackheath after breakfast. Mr. Fisher and the Count accompany me through the Park to Greenwich Hospital. Stop there to see the New Chapel; admittance one shilling. This universally reckoned a masterpiece, both in point of architecture, sculpture, and painting. Beautiful columns of marble, with bases and capitals of the Corinthian order. The Apostles, the history pieces, the sculptured ceiling, the seating, the floor, the marble table at the altar, the Altar-piece itself, viz., The Shipwreck of St. Paul at Malta, done by the celebrated West, are all admirable.—Take leave of the Count and my friend. Step again into the Greenwich stage-coach, which sets me down about one o'clock p.m. at the Obelisk, St.

---

[1] In his *Chronicles of Greenwich* (London, 1886), Mr. L'Estrange makes a passing reference (vol. ii., p. 175 *n.*) to 'Sir Gregory Page, who had built a grand house in Blackheath Park. This park contained 284 acres, with trees "scattered and clumped with pleasing negligence." The splendid furniture, verd antique tables, pier-glasses, Persian carpets, busts by Rysbrack, Sèvres porcelain, pictures, etc., which cost £90,000, were sold in 1782, and the park cut up for building.'

George's Fields, near Blackfriars Bridge. Go in here to Sir Ashton Lever's Museum, where spend two hours. This the finest collection in Europe, arranged in the most orderly and kept in the most cleanly manner. An inexhaustible fund of entertainment to the naturalist. But it would require days, and weeks, and months, to review it to perfection.

Arrive at four p.m. at Miss French's, Dover Street, where dine, and pass the afternoon in the most agreeable manner.—Walk through the King's Park in the evening to Mr. Ritchie's, who introduces me to a Lieutenant Murray lately arrived from the Continent. He gives us some interesting anecdotes concerning this eventful war. Return to Oxford Street to supper.

Friday, 31st July. London.—Set out in the morning with Mr. Brodie and a Mr. Best, along Holborn. Visit the different departments of the Bank of England, that wonderful centre of business, where so many millions of money are counted and transferred every day in the space of two hours, viz., from eleven a.m. to one p.m. From the Bank proceed to the Tower. Enter first the Spanish Armoury. See many spoils of the famous Armada, &c. Here see also a noble statue of Queen Elizabeth at full length, and in her armour, with her horse and her page, all standing in a majestic and striking attitude. Pass under the Bloody Tower. Shown next into the Horse Armoury. Infinite number here of complete suits of armour, coats-of-mail, helmets, cuirasses, &c., as worn by heroes of old. The kings of England, down from William the Conquerer to his present Majesty, are all here in armour and mounted on horseback. From this apartment we are conducted next into the large hall below the Foot Armoury. In this Hall there is complete harness for six thousand horses, all new and in good order. From this hall ascend to the Foot Armoury; a spacious hall, full of guns, swords, pistols, &c., arranged in the most elegant order, and kept in the cleanliest manner, ready for immediate service.

Leave the Tower, and direct our course to Finsbury Square and *Lackington's Temple of the Muses.* This the largest stationery shop in the world. A rotundo with five stories of books, rising one above another by five flights of stairs, the cupola lighted from the top. From this rotundo rooms extend on each side, with different assortments of books, and different offices for different purposes, &c. The building itself is like a palace. The cheapest books here in Europe.

Proceed next to the Royal Exchange, where so many men from so many nations of the world meet every lawful day on business; and individuals of each description are to be found at once in their own particular department of the Exchange, so that in seeming confusion there is here the greatest order. This the case also at the Bank of England.—Visit next Guildhall.

Thence to Furnival's Inn, and others of the Inns of Court. Visit Mr. James Chambers, Attorney. Pass the afternoon with him. Walk with him through different parts of the town in the evening. Part with him at Cleveland Row; and return to Oxford Street to supper.

Saturday, 1st August. London.—Rainy day. Go to see *Merlin's Museum*, a most wonderful display of human ingenuity. A vast variety of most curious movements, depending upon electrical and magnetical principles. The mechanical powers exhibited here in the greatest perfection.

Mr. Fisher comes in from Blackheath, and dines with me. Having prevailed with him to stay with me all night, he and I sit up till two in the morning, revising his translation of Count Duroure's poem on the French Revolution.

Sunday, 2nd August. Richmond and Kew.—Walk up to Kew. The Gardens not being open, go into the Pleasure-Ground. See here a prodigy of nature, the *Kangaroo* from Botany Bay. This animal, like the Opossum, carries and defends its young in a pouch under its belly. It hops with amazing agility on its two hinder legs, which are exceedingly long and strong compared with its fore legs, which are short and weak. Its tail, which is also very long, seems to serve the animal both as a balance and as a rudder. It is fearful as the roe, and about the size of a fawn. It seems to belong to the rat-kind. There are seven of them here, and they have propagated since they were brought home. Besides the Kangaroo, there are other curious creatures shown here at the Royal menagerie: Such as the buffalo from India,—the bull, the ox, the cow and the calf of this animal,—all thriving very well. There are also some very beautiful birds, such as the white silver pheasant-cock of China. He has a very strong bill and long spurs, and is a very irascible bird and a good fighter. There are here also the Curassou Cock and hen from the Island of that name. The hen is very nearly as beautiful as the cock, an uncommon circumstance in the feathered tribes.

Walk up to Richmond Bridge. Vast numbers of London barges come up with the tide. Among the rest two superbly decorated Barges, carrying some of the Lords of the Admiralty and some ladies of quality along with them. These barges are finely gilt, have rich canopies, covering a nice apartment with elegant tables and beautiful seats with velvet cushions, having the Arms of the Admiralty on their stern.—Saunter up to Richmond Hill, and along Richmond Park. See here a glorious prospect of London and its vicinity. Count here upwards of thirty spires. St. Paul's and Westminster Abbey are here very conspicuous objects, about ten miles distant. The view from Richmond Hill up the Thames by Twickenham, &c., is beyond expression fine.

Come down by the river-side. A grand view of Sion House, a magnificent seat of the Duke of

Northumberland, on the opposite side of the river. This much more like a palace than the King's Palace at Kew.—By the side of the Thames, betwixt Richmond Bridge and Kew Bridge, find a good many rare plants.

Heavy rain falls upon me, and drenches me to the skin. Here muse upon the life and death of Thomson. He died in consequence of an excursion from London to Richmond in 1748, and is buried in Richmond Church. The sweet Verses which Collins wrote on his death here recur to my remembrance in all their beauty and energy.

> ' In yonder grave a Druid lies,
>   Where slowly winds the stealing wave ;
> The year's best sweets shall duteous rise,
>   To deck its poet's sylvan grave.
>
> ' In yon deep bed of whispering reeds
>   His airy harp shall now be laid—
> That he whose heart in sorrow bleeds,
>   May love thro' life the soothing shade,' &c.

Get comfortable lodgings all night at Kew.

Monday, 3rd August.—Find admission at Kew Gardens at ten o'clock. Introduce myself to Mr. Aiton. He shows me the first Collection of plants I ever saw, both indigenous and exotic. Mr. Aiton favours me with specimens of the following rare plants: *Lepidium alpinum, Erinus alpinus, Scrophularia aquatica* (a rare variety from Yorkshire), *Scutellaria minor, Asperula Cynanchica, Gentiana Pneumonanthe, Lythrum hyssopifolium, Campanula pumila, C. patula, Bapleurum rotundi-*

folium, Sedum Anglicum, Saxifraga Hirculus, Silene quinquevulnera, Papaver Cambricum, Bryonia nigra, &c.

Leave Kew in the afternoon. Stop at Turnamgreen to refresh. At Hammersmith regale on fruits. Walk through Kensington Park, home through Hyde Park. Observe some roach and pike in the Serpentine river. Sup with Mr. George Brodie and a Mr. Cockburn of the *Phœnix* E. Indiaman.

Tuesday, 4th August. London.—Rainy morning. At mid-day go out and call upon Miss Maria French. From Dover Street proceed by the Green Park to Sloane Street. Dine with my old friend Mr. Robert Bissett. No company with him but his wife and daughter, little Catherine. Spend the afternoon there very comfortably. Walk up with them in the evening to Hyde Park. Return at nine p.m. to my lodgings.

Wednesday, 5th August. London.—Meet by appointment at two p.m., at the Spring Garden Coffee-house, my friends Messrs. Bissett, Fisher, Robinson; the latter on the eve of being married to a Miss Lewis. Conversation on the subject of potatoes. Conversation on the subject of Count Duroure's Poem. Receive a present of the Count's *Epithalame* on the marriage of the Prince and Princess of Wales.

Walk out to St. James's Park. Part there with my friends, and go to Dover Street and dine with Miss Maria French. After dinner walk out with her to Green Park; thence to Hyde Park; thence to the Mall. Drink tea at Mr. Forsyth's, Kensington, and see his curious cabinet of shells, fossils, plants, &c. Introduced here to a Mr. Mason, botanist, from the Cape of Good Hope and St. Helena. Conversation with Mr. Forsyth about my brother Thomas.

Messrs. Mason and Forsyth convey [? convoy] us to the Mall. Return in the evening with Miss Maria to Dover Street. After parting with her, go in on my way to Oxford Street to the White Horse inn. There fall in with two French refugees. Conversation was concerning the present state of things.

Thursday, 6th August. London.—Went down to St. James's Palace, and from the Guard-room had a fine view of the shifting of the Guards. After which went down to Parade. Then to Captain Mackay's, whom I found at home. Called upon Mr. Ritchie, who accompanies me again to Westminster Abbey. See all the Tombs, King Henry the Seventh's Chapel, the images of the kings and queens in waxwork, &c.

Those of the Tombs that seem to display most originality of genius and the best taste, are Nightingale's; Hargreave's, Esq.; General Fleming's; General Wade's; Handel's; Sir Isaac Newton's.—On the famous Duke of Buckingham's is the following epitaph :

> Dubius, sed non improbus vixi ;
> Incertus morior, non perturbatus ;
> Humanum est nescire et errare :

>Deo confido
>Omnipotenti, benevolentissimo :
>Ens entium, miserere mei.

From our contemplations among the Tombs (which are so well calculated to impress the mind with seriousness and awe), we direct our steps next to the House of Commons, and next to the House of Lords.—Having spent some time in this great national Senate-house, we take a long walk through different departments of this vast Metropolis, till being fatigued with heat we stop before dinner, and regale ourselves with a variety of ripe fruits about Covent-garden market; from which we go in to the Three Tun[s] Tavern and dine, and repose after dinner till six p.m. About half-past six go to Haymarket Theatre, and see young Bannister in the part of *Colonel Feignwell* in the Comedy of *A Bold Stroke for a Wife*. The theatre crowded. Bannister plays his part with much dexterity and propriety, and gives much satisfaction through every part of the Play.— After the play, part with Ritchie in Piccadilly, and make the best of my way home by New Bond Street.

Friday, 7th August. London.—Breakfast with Captain Mackay, No. 16, Fludyer Street. The Captain a plain, good-natured, hospitable man. See there Dr. Braid from St. Andrews. The Doctor here on very good bread; employed in inspecting the recruits for the army. Informed here that the Duke of Atholl's Mankse Regiment is very nearly completed. Dr. Braid says he has inspected and passed in the course of the four last days no less than thirty-seven recruits for that regiment alone.

After breakfast take leave of the good honest Captain, who gives me commissions to be carried to Sheffield. Wait upon Mr. Humphrey Donaldson, Whitehall. Have the pleasure of seeing there Mrs. Maxwell from Dunkeld.—Go next to Soho Square, No. 12, Denmark Street, and call upon Mr. Forbes, bookseller. From Soho proceed immediately by Piccadilly and Hyde Park Corner to Sloane Street, and dine again with my good friend Mr. Robert Bissett, where spend the afternoon; and after having had an evening walk with Mr. and Mrs. Bissett, return to Oxford Street to supper.

Saturday, 8th August. London.—Call in the forenoon at Dr. Smith's, Great Marlborough Street.[1] The Doctor not yet returned from Norwich. Disappointed therefore in not seeing the Linnæan Herbarium. From Great Marlborough Street proceed to Mr. James Chambers', Attorney, Lamb's Conduit Street. Mrs. Chambers just brought to bed of a daughter, and in a safe way of recovery.—Meet Mr. Bissett. Go with him to call upon Dr. W. Thomson in —— ——. The Doctor not in town. Meet Mr. Fisher at ——

---

[1] Dr. Smith, of Norwich, afterwards Sir J. E. Smith, was the founder of the Linnean Society, which now possesses the Herbarium above referred to, being Linnæus' own collection, purchased by Dr. Smith.

Coffee house. Call upon Mr. Ritchie at Barton Street. Dine with Messrs. Bissett and Fisher at the Blue Posts Tavern, Russell Street, near Covent Garden. Pass the afternoon together in conversing over old scenes. Part with my two friends. Return home.

Sunday, 9th August. London.—Breathe the pure morning air in Hyde Park. Walk through Kensington Gardens to Mr. Forsyth's, where breakfast. Go to church with the family. After church visit flower and fruit-gardens. Mr. Forsyth has great merit for his method of renewing old trees and increasing the quantity and quality of the fruit. Introduced at dinner to a Mr. Frazer and a Mr. Allan, both great botanical characters from the West Indies and America. Walk up-stairs to review Mr. Forsyth's Cabinet. Mr. Forsyth, Junior, gives me some fine specimens of new plants from Botany Bay. Take with me a list of Alpine plants wanted from Scotland for Kensington. Drink tea with the family, and take my leave of them in the evening.

Monday, 10th August.—Rise at six o'clock a.m., and pack up for my departure. Leave Mr. Brodie's at seven, and arrive at eight at the Green Dragon, Bishopsgate, where set my foot on board of the Cambridge stage-coach.

Leave London. Look back with an indescribable mixture of feelings on this vast Metropolis, well termed 'a world of wonders in itself.' Think on all I have seen, and suffered, and enjoyed, in the City and its environs. Ruminate on its magnificence; its extent; its populousness; its riches; its poverty; its dissipation; its luxuries; its vanities; its vices; its virtues.

Roll on through a beautiful country; and lose sight of the smoke of London. Breakfast at Hoddeston.[1] Hay harvest not done here yet, on account of the rains. Some fields of rye cut down. Some fields of wheat almost ready. Hear of some fields of wheat cut down in several places in the neighbourhood. Great outcry among the people for want of bread. God send peace and a plentiful crop, and a good harvest! At Ware pass the New River that supplies London.

[1] Hoddesdon—seventeen miles from London at that date, the measurement being taken from Shoreditch Church. (See Paterson's *Itinerary*.)

CHAPTER VII.

Cambridge—Burleigh—Doncaster—Sheffield revisited—Leeds—Harrogate.

MONDAY, 10th August.—Dine at the Angel inn, Barkway.[1] Betwixt that and Cambridge (an open, dry, chalky country; much fallowing for wheat; they sow the Red kind generally here;) observe at times from the top of my vehicle some rare plants by the way-side, such as the *Campanula glomerata, C. patula, Asperula Cynanchica,* &c., &c.

Arrive at Cambridge at five p.m. After drinking coffee, take a walk through the courts of several of the colleges.

Tuesday, 11th August. Cambridge.—No coach sets out for the North till to-morrow. After breakfast, make a botanical excursion to the Gogmagog Hills, about four miles south from Cambridge. Find there a good number of rare plants, such as *Athamanta Libanotis, Asperula Cynanchica, Campanula glomerata, Caucalis daucoides, Carduus acaulis, Carlina vulgaris, Ononis*

[1] About thirty-four miles from London.

spinosa, Centaurea calcitrapa, Gentiana autumnalis, Hedysarum Onobrychis, Linum perenne, Melampyrum pratense, Cucubalus Otites, &c., &c., but do not find *Ophrys* ——. The country here all chalk, with flinty nodules imbedded in it.

Return in the afternoon to visit the University. The King's Chapel in King's College, founded by Henry VI., forwarded by Henry VII., and finished by Henry VIII., one of the most complete things of the kind in the world, and the admiration of all who have seen it. The Painting above the Altar is a striking representation of the taking down of our Saviour's body from the Cross. The paintings on the windows are admirable: the fretting of the roof beyond expression beautiful: the organs a masterpiece. The floor of the finest marble: the roof seemingly supported upon nothing. Eleven places on each side without terminate each in a high top or spire, besides the towers and spires at each corner of the building, forming in all twenty-six spires, give the external side of the building a very singular and striking appearance. The emblematical carved figures within allude to the Roses, to the Houses of York and Lancaster.

After seeing King's College go next to Trinity College. The Chapel here also magnificent. The Altar-piece represents the Angel Michael treading Satan under his feet, and going to bind him in chains. The attitude of Michael is inexpressibly dignified. But the most remarkable object here is the Statue of Sir Isaac Newton, supposed to be exceedingly like him. It is of the finest wrought marble exalted upon a high pedestal. He holds a prism in his hand, and stands in graceful but thoughtful attitude, as if studying the refraction of the rays of light from a cloud during the time of the rainbow. His observatory is a stately tower. Next visit St. John's College, &c., &c., till dark. The river Cam waters this place.

Wednesday, 12th August. Cambridge.—At five a.m. (an excessive degree of heat) take leave with regret of this venerable Seat of literature, bid adieu to these 'antique spires that crown the watery glade.' Set forward aboard the coach to Huntingdon to breakfast. Hay-harvest not done. Some rye cut down. Vast fields of beans. Beautiful willows. See near Huntingdon the *Sagittaria sagittifolia.* From Huntingdon proceed to Stilton. Near Stilton have a view of Wittlesea-meer, famous for tench. From thence to Stamford, where dine in a great company of travellers from different parts of England. A character; a lady from Ireland. Stop here to see Burleigh, the Earl of Exeter's. Set out after dinner for Burleigh. This justly esteemed one of the first Seats in England. The trees of the park are venerable for their age and size, and disposed in the most beautiful and tasty manner. The place extensive and magnificent. A noble canal, with a bridge over it, winds through the Park, containing a variety of fish. The lawn covered with Spanish sheep, differing essentially from ours both in shape and colour. Very prolific, and very good mutton; of various colours; long white tails, the bodies speckled, black and blue; horns somewhat resembling those of goats. The ewes have frequently two lambs at a birth.

Burleigh (built in 1585 by the then Earl of that name) more resembles a Royal palace than an Earl's chateau. A hollow square, containing a large narrow court, enclosed with turreted buildings; the rooms not remarkably large, but adorned with paintings the finest of any in England, some of them the finest in Europe. Works of the greatest Italian masters here; endless variety. Those that catch the attention of Connoisseurs most are Dominicino's Mistress by himself; three paintings on a glass window; the Holy Family by Carlo Dolci, for which the Earl of Exeter paid one thousand five hundred pounds Sterling; but above all, Christ Blessing the Bread, by the same hand, for which the present Earl has been offered six thousand pounds, but will not part with it for any money; it is perhaps one of the first Paintings in the world.

Return in the evening to Stamford. The weather still continues intolerably hot. The climate of the south of England is very sensibly hotter than that of Perthshire. I have been in a constant state of perspiration for upwards of three weeks.

Thursday, 13th August. Stamford.—Get up early in expectation of a place in the Mail coach at seven o'clock. Two Mails arrive, but the places all occupied. Obliged to wait here till ten a.m. Heavy coach arrives at ten; have a berth on board. Set out from Stamford (finely situated on the north bank of the river Welland); easy ascent of several miles to Wytham-common. A great deal of the hay-harvest not over here. Fine high, open, healthy country. Good deal of pasture-ground; the farms here not remarkably well cultivated. Arrive at Grantham to dinner. One lady and eleven gentlemen, dine all together; hearty entertainment. Two English clergymen; a Swiss gentleman. Set out all in company; six on board, and six in the hold.[1] From a rising-ground to the north of Grantham have a most extensive and rich prospect, towards Lincoln Abbey. See here a great part of the boundless plains of Nottinghamshire, Lincolnshire, &c. At Newark pass the river Trent. Observe the *Sagittaria sagittifolia*, and in one place the *Jasione*, which I had not seen a plant of for several hundreds of miles; but these stage-coaches are a bad business for botanists. Travel through an

---

[1] It would be interesting to know whether this nautical way of referring to stage-coach travelling, of which the above is not the first instance, was a peculiarity of the diarist's, or whether it was a common usage at that time. In the latter event, the similar custom in the United States at the present day ought probably to be regarded as a survival from the eighteenth century.

opulent corn country waving ripe for harvest. Extensive farms well-cultivated; though in many places grass 'bauks'[1] and crooked ridges, which a Scotch farmer would laugh at. Few oats; many beans; much wheat and barley. Come to Tuxford.[2] Here part with our lady and her husband, a clergyman and his wife of this place. Night comes upon us as we approach to the boundary of Yorkshire. Few houses by the wayside: these large farms depopulate the country. A good deal of lightning; no rain however. Calm, warm evening, with high clouds, the stars dimly twinkling through the gloom. At Bawtry enter Yorkshire. Pass over a desert common. Dark: converse about robbers: no guard attends us: all of us unarmed. Arrive at Doncaster at eleven p.m., thank God, without any untoward accident having befallen us. Sup, ten gentlemen together. At threequarters past eleven, the coach sets forward with my fellow-travellers, whom I recommend to the protection of Heaven, and rest here all night in a good comfortable inn.

Friday, 14th August. Doncaster.—Slept soundly for eight hours at the Angel Inn, one of the best inns in England. Rise and dress before breakfast. After breakfast, walk out through the town, view the market-place, and admire the neatness and cleanliness of the streets, houses, &c. Don-

---

[1] Strips of uncultivated ground between the furrows; equivalent to the 'doles' or 'dools' of Bailey's *Dictionary*.
[2] Twelve miles beyond Newark.

caster supposed by travellers to be among the neatest towns in England. The public buildings in general have their date marked on their front, together with the name of the reigning magistrate at the time of their erection. Walk into the church-yard. The Church a stately gothic building having a magnificent square tower with sixteen points a-top. The doors being open, and the church now a-repairing, have a view of its inside. Fine set of organs. No paintings on the windows. On the left hand of the altar-piece is inscribed the Lord's Prayer in large golden letters; on the right hand the Creed in the same; and in the middle betwixt them the Ten Commandments in the same characters, a rising sun above with I.H.S. in its centre. In the adjoining aisles are several pretty marble monuments with good Latin inscriptions. The church is well paved, well seated, simple and unornamented, but kept clean, swept and garnished. Fine music bells here. How different in general, and how exceedingly superior are the English churches to our poor Scotch kirks!

Take a walk across the bridge and along the banks of the river. The Dun or Don, from which the town has its name, is the same stream that runs by Sheffield. It has a little pleasant fall here, about one hundred yards above the bridge. A waterfall is a rare object indeed in most parts of the east and south counties of England. Below the bridge on the north bank of the river observe the *Sisymbrium sylvestre.*—Good market for corn here, beans, oats, rye, barley, wheat. The price of wheat fallen here twelve shillings a quarter within these three days; at present thirty-six shillings the three bushels.

Send up my luggage to the Rein-Deer Inn at two p.m. to wait the Sheffield coach. Dine there with three gentlemen of the neighbourhood. Informed by one of them that there had been a dreadful storm through the night, thunder, lightning, and rain. Set out from Doncaster at four p.m. Fine prospect of a fine country all the way to Sheffield. First, a little to the northwest of Doncaster, *Cusworth* (Rightson,[1] Esq.): Second, *Sprotsbro'* (Earl Kinnoul): Third, *Cumsboro'*, a curious old Castle of an hexagonal form, situated on a woody eminence on the south bank of the river Don.[2] Much limestone burnt here, and carried up to Sheffield, &c. Fourth, Squire Finch's Castle.[3] From a rising-ground here have a view of, Fifth, *Wentworth*, the Seat of Earl Fitzwilliam, opposite on the north bank of the river. The grounds here on each side finely diversified into hill and valley. Sixth, *Aldric Hall* :[4] Seventh, Jo.

[1] In Paterson's *Itinerary* the name is 'Wrighston, Esqr.' Evidently a mistake of a letter has been made in each case, and the name ought to be 'Wrightson.'
[2] This is evidently the 'Conisbrough' of Paterson's *Itinerary*, and the 'Coningsburgh' of *Ivanhoe*. (In the descriptive account appended to the novel, *Note L*, Scott quotes from Gough's edition of Camden's *Britannia*, 2nd edit., vol. iii., p. 267.)
[3] 'On right, Savile Finch, Esq.' (Paterson's *Itinerary*).
[4] 'Aldwark, Foljamb, Esq.' (Paterson's *Itinerary*).

Walker's, Esq., beautifully situated on a height on the south bank of the Don, near Rother[h]am. Stop at Rotheram and refresh. After passing Rotheram about a mile, look back on the town with its church and spire, forming a fine object in the landscape. The rain falls heavy upon us. Go inside and arrive at Sheffield half-past seven p.m. Go in to the Tontine, and get Captain Stewart's account of the Riots. Order up my things to Sharrow, and arrive in the evening at the hospitable mansion of my friend.[1]

Saturday, 15th August. Sharrow.—Go down to Sheffield with Mr. Mackenzie, and view Mr. Alsop's Iron-works; particularly his method of making anvils. Afterwards go to the Coffee-house, and visit Captains Stewart, McDonald, and McKilligan. See the billiard-room. Take a walk through the market-place, &c.; and return to Sharrow to dinner. Company at dinner, Colonel Cameron of the Sheffield Regiment, Captains Stewart and McDonald, Messrs. Preston and Shaldwick. Walk down in the evening again to town. Introduced to Mr. Grieve at his house. Play at backgammon. Sup, and return to Sharrow.

Sunday, 16th August. Sharrow.—Go to St. Paul's Church, the church of my friend. Mr. Goodwin, a young man, reads prayers in the forenoon, and my friend preaches. The same in the afternoon. Dine at the good old lady Mrs. Smith's, my friend's

---

[1] The Rev. Mr. Mackenzie, with whom the diarist had spent several days (July 13 to July 20) during his southward journey.

mother-in-law. Drink tea at Mr. Preston's. After tea, attend evening service in the Town Church, where Mr. Preston preaches a sermon on Death. Sup at his house, and return late to Sharrow.

Monday, 17th August. Sheffield.—Went with Mr. Mackenzie to the Button-manufacture carried on to a great extent here by Mr. —— and Co. The different processes shown us, and described to us with great precision and clearness by one of the Company. After seeing this very ingenious manufacture, walk to the Tontine tavern, and dine there with the Mess; Colonel Cameron, Captains Stewart, McDonald, McKilligan, Lieutenant Radcliffe, Agnew, &c.

In the afternoon, Mr. Downs, chaplain to the Sheffield volunteers, conducts me to see the Plating-works. The slitting of the steel, &c., all performed by wonderful mechanism indeed, the machines driven by the power of steam. In the evening go to the Parade. After Parade, receive their commissions for the North.[1] Mr. Mackenzie and I go to supper to Mr. Preston's. An agreeable party; music, vocal and instrumental. After supper, return to Sharrow.

Tuesday, 18th August.—Breakfast at Sharrow with my worthy friend and his amiable young family. Bless them, and part with them. Mr. Mackenzie himself accompanies me to Sheffield.

[1] In these days of cheap postage and parcel post one is apt to forget that, even long after the date of this diary, friends were accustomed to oblige each other as far as possible by carrying letters and messages to distant relatives.

Go in to a cutler's shop and purchase razors, knives, &c. Afterwards go to see the manufacture of iron fenders and grates. This also a rare work. Go next to purchase some scissars for little presents. Sheffield the first town for cutlery-work perhaps in the world. Adieu to Sheffield. It is a dirty, monotonous town, but surrounded with one of the finest countries in England: romantic dales, sweetly-rising hills, plantations, enclosures, and neat gentlemen's seats on every side.

Mr. Mackenzie conveys [? convoys] me as far as the third mile-stone nearly from Sheffield;[1] and there introduces me to the house of Booth, Esq., of Brush-house. Mr. Booth a very ingenious man. His place well laid out and finely situated. His hedges, stone-fences, and plantations all a model. His neighbours are obliged to him for his good example of improvement. Mr. Booth also a very capital mechanic and mathematician. Shews us a very fine camera-clara, and a most ingenious equatorial made by Ramsden. Explains its construction and powers most concisely and distinctly. Entertains us with a forenoon-luncheon. Here we part with him. And here I part with my worthy and generous friend Mr. Mackenzie; whose hospitality and friendly offices have contributed much to the pleasure I derive from this long and wide excursion. May Heaven befriend

[1] Although the diarist does not definitely say so, he was once more astride of the horse which had brought him south from Perthshire, and which he had left at Sharrow on July 20, continuing his journey to London by coach.

him at all times! Arrive at the Bank-top inn about one o'clock p.m. Stop here to refresh myself and horse, as well as to contemplate for a little the charming view seen from the top of this hill, commanding a widely-extended horizon all round, a rich well-cultivated country, interspersed with 'hill and dale, and wood and lawn and spire, and glittering towns and gilded streams.' Wentworth Castle, the seat of the Earl of Stafford, lies about a mile and a half south-west of this curious eminence, and the place and the park about it make a fine appearance here. On this hill his Lordship has erected a long line of artificial ruins, somewhat resembling an old fortified wall with turrets, which must produce a very noble effect seen from Wentworth Castle.

Set out after dinner, and pass through Barnsl[e]y, a considerable town. From Barnsly proceed to Wakefield, and stop in the afternoon. As you enter to Wakefield from the south a beautiful sight [? seat] presents itself on your right hand on a high wooded elevation. This is Heath, the supposed 'Choice' of Pomfret the poet.[1] The river Kelder passes by Wakefield, and a canal goes from hence to Halifax, carrying coals, corn, &c.

Wakefield, an elegant well-situated town, with

[1] 'Near some fair town I'd have a private seat,
    Built uniform, not little, nor too great;
    Better, if on a rising ground it stood;
    On this side fields, on that a neighbouring wood.'
        (From *The Choice*, by John Pomfret.)

a fine Spire, and some beautiful streets. A new town is begun to be erected on the north side of the old, and a new church on an [?] exclusive site. The country hereabout most delightful; and the harvest just approaching. Wheat has fallen here within these few days from three guineas the three bushels to twenty-seven shillings. After leaving Wakefield, proceed through a fine rich coal country to the banks of the Air[e], a fine river, bringing up considerable small craft, with corn, &c., and carrying down vast quantities of broadcloth, &c., from Leeds. Arrive at Leeds in the dusk.

Wednesday, 19th August. Leeds.—This a very large populous town, finely situated on the north bank of the river Air. It is remarkable for the broad-cloth manufacture, and is in this respect among the first towns in England. The ground rises by an easy ascent for several miles as you go north from Leeds. About two miles to the north of the town stands Gladder, an elegant seat of Dickson, Esq.[1] About seven miles to the north of Leeds come to Harwood, a cleanly little village, and in its immediate vicinity on your left-hand Harwood-house (Lord Harwood, formerly Lascelles),[2] a most beautiful Seat on a finely-rising

---

[1] 'Allerton Gledhow. Dixon Esq.' (Paterson's *Itinerary*).
[2] In Paterson's *Itinerary*, published ten years before the date of the Diary, the entry is, 'Harewood house, Edwin Lascelles, Esq.' This Mr. Lascelles was raised to the peerage in 1790, as 'Lord Harewood, of Harewood Castle, co. York.' He died without issue on January 25, 1795, when

bank, laid out in elegant taste; and below the house a large piece of water, forming one of the finest ponds anywhere to be seen. The grounds rise charmingly to the south and north of this basin, and are richly decked with venerable trees and well-disposed plantations.

After leaving Harwood, come down to the bank of the river Wharf[e], a delightful stream here. Pass the Wharf, and breakfast at the Ship Inn at the north end of the bridge.[1] Leave the bank of the Wharf, and pass along a delightful well-cultivated tract of country in company with two travelling gentlemen; one of them of Leeds, well acquainted with the country, and very intelligent and communicative. Beautifully rising grounds on each side of the Wharf. Arrive at Knaresborough Forest, some time ago begun to be cultivated and enclosed by the direction of the Earl of Bute. The grounds here hilly, heathy and poor. Arrive at

HARROWGATE.

High Harrowgate contains three capital inns, with very large rooms, and numerous accom-

---

the barony expired; but his heir-at-law, Edward Lascelles, Esq. (great-grandfather of the present Earl of Harewood), was made 'Baron Harewood, of Harewood, co. York,' on June 18, 1796 (*Burke*). There was thus no existing Lord Harewood when the diarist passed Harewood House on August 19, 1795.

[1] The Ship Inn, nine miles from Leeds, was evidently a well-known coaching inn, as it is marked in Paterson's *Itinerary*.

modations for strangers. The Dragon Inn, the
Granby, the Queen's Head, &c. In the Queen's
Head there is a room that dines with ease one
hundred and twenty persons with fifty servants
attending. The houses all crowded at present
with Company at the Waters. Here is also a
very elegant Theatre, fit to contain fifty people
[on the stage], with pit and pit-boxes, boxes and
gallery. The Company here have frequently
Plays, both public and private. When there is to
be a public Play, cards are sent to the different
houses to give notice to the Company.—Take up
my quarters at Low Harrowgate, just in the
vicinity of the Spaw. Here are also a great
number of commodious inns· for the company
during the watering season, which continues from
June to the end of September. Some people continue here all the year round, and think that the
waters produce the most powerful effects during
hard frost.

The water here is very strongly impregnated
with sulphur and salt, and is esteemed the best
mineral in Europe, especially for scorbutic complaints. Its virtues were not discovered till about
sixty years ago by the landlord of one of the neigh-
bouring houses, who recommended it to a lady of
quality much afflicted with the scurvy, who upon
drinking it for two months was miraculously
cured; and hence arose at first the character of
the water. Buildings were immediately erected;
and every year since it has been more and more

8—2

frequented with people from every quarter, and has produced many wonderful cures, on weak, nervous, scorbutic habits, &c. The water somewhat resembles that of the Well at Moffat, but is much more strongly impregnated. Three English pints taken in the morning, at about a fourth of an hour's interval, are supposed to be the medium dose; but the requisite quantity depends much on the habit and complaint of the patient. There are baths also kept at about the temperature of 70°. Bathing produces very powerful good effects; and when the patient takes the bath less drinking is required.—Dr. Hutchison of High Harrowgate and another apothecary generally attend here, and direct the company as to their regimen. The use of spirituous liquors is prohibited; and a little malt liquor or a little wine and water is what is generally used at meals.

After dinner walk up to the moors on the west of Harrowgate. The prospect from the high grounds is extensive (see York Cathedral twenty-two miles off), and rich towards the north-east and south-east; but towards the west it is wild as many of our Scottish moors, covered with heath interspersed with the Reindeer lichen, the *Lycopodium Selago, Scirpus cæspitosus,* and other plants common on our Scottish moors. Here also I find the *Lycopodium inundatum,* and *Lysimachia tenella,* &c.—Join a number of gentlemen at supper, and get some information with respect to the company just now at the waters.

Thursday, 20th August. Harrowgate.—Rise in the morning at six a.m., and drink the waters; then ascend the moors again, and inhale the heathy healthy breeze till nine o'clock; after which breakfast heartily. About nine have a fine view of the company at the wells. Harrowgate but a poor place in winter. The inhabitants live chiefly by what they get from the company in summer. No burning coal within sixteen miles of the place. —Set out at mid-day for York. Arrive at Knaresborough, situated on a rocky bank of the river Nid. In passing the bridge have a fine view of Cobhal Hall, the seat of Sir John Cobhal.[1] Pass through Knaresborough and descend into the plain country of Yorkshire.

Arrive at Thornton-rail (Colonel Thornton's), formerly the Seat of the Duke of York, finely situated on a rising ground; a fine new garden a little to the south of the house on the declivity of the eminence. At three o'clock p.m. come to Green-Hammerton, where dine. Fall in here with a gentleman of Macclesfield in Cheshire, who informs me that about his place land setts [*i.e.* lets] at eight pounds an acre; knew some there have been offered ten pounds. At Hammerton-green oats sell at present at half a guinea a bushel (Cheshire bushel forty-five pounds). Wheat sold

[1] A mistake (made, perhaps, in transliterating from the original shorthand) for 'Coghill.' Paterson's *Itinerary* has 'Coghill hall, Coghill, Esq.'; but the baronetcy dates from 1778, and the first Baronet was succeeded in 1790 by his son, Sir John Coghill (*Burke*).

here lately at four guineas per Quarter, equal to eight bushels. Great fall of grain every where in this country of late. The corn-dealers detected in their tricks in endeavouring to persuade the farmers to keep up their grain in hopes of an exorbitant price. Leave Green-Hammerton at four p.m. This gentleman travels with me to York.

CHAPTER VIII.

York—Castle Howard—The North Riding of Yorkshire.

*T*HURSDAY, 20th August.—In the vicinity of York harvest begun. Oats, barley, wheat, &c., cut down. Fine farming here, and excellent crops. All the turnips of England (almost all I have yet seen) are sown in the broadcast;[1] the potatoes are drilled; the wheat used about York is both of the red and white sort.—Plants I observed betwixt Knaresborough and York: Plenty of *Eupatorium cannabinum, Epilobium hirsutum, Scrophularia aquatica, Betonica*

[1] From this remark one is led to infer that the diarist was accustomed to see turnips sown in drills. The cultivation of turnips in the open fields had only been begun in Scotland about fifty years previously, and the seed had been sown broadcast until 1753, in which year a Roxburghshire farmer (William Dawson, referred to more specially on pp. 156, 157, *post*) introduced the practice of sowing in drills, the result of experience gained by him in Yorkshire and Essex. The superiority of the new system being speedily recognised, a complete revolution was thus effected in Scottish turnip-culture, and, to judge from the above reference in the Diary, the farmers of Scotland had then wholly adopted the more scientific method, while the majority of their English brethren still lagged behind.

officinalis, Bryonia nigra, Convolvulus sepium, C. arvensis, some of *Jasione montana* near Hammerton, where also I observed *Nepeta Cataria.* Betwixt Knaresborough and Green-Hammerton I gathered *Campanula Trachelium,* &c.—About four miles from York, the Cathedral appears not above a mile from you. Approach York about six p.m. The river Ouse runs gently by the town, and besides small craft, it bears up to the city some vessels in the merchant-way of two masts, but of no great burden. A canal sets off from the Ouse towards the north, and carries coals and other articles of trade up the country for a considerable extent. A great line of canal is to form a junction betwixt the Humber and Liverpool.

Walk out in the evening to see the Cathedral, one of the greatest and finest in the world. Its length five hundred, twenty-four and a half feet; its breadth two hundred and twenty-two feet. The largest Quire I have yet seen. The great Window seventy-five feet high by thirty-two feet wide. The paintings of this and indeed of all the windows of this vast building are wonderfully grand. In the body of the Quire are the seats of the Judges in the times of Assize on the one hand, and on the other side is the seat of the Archbishop, and to the left of it the seat of the Lord Mayor, &c.

Go next into the Outer Vestry, where among other pieces of antiquity, you see the wooden chests, *one thousand four hundred years old,* where the priestly robes were kept. Here also you see a very ingenious wooden model of the Cathedral, made by a little boy of this city with his knife, &c.—Were next conducted into the Inner Vestry, and shewn a great number of very old curiosities, and among the rest a large Bugle-horn, given in a donation to the Archbishop of York by Ulphus, one of the West Saxon kings. It was taken away in the wars betwixt the Houses of York and Lancaster, and restored afterwards to the Cathedral. Here is shewn also the cloak of James VI.; and also the silver pastoral staff presented to the Archbishop of York by Catharine of Spain, mother-in-law to Charles II.; &c.

In the next place were shewn to the Chancel, where there are several well-finished monuments of marble erected to the memory of illustrious persons. Among these is to be remarked the monument of Sir George Sackville, by Fisher of this city. The statue of Sir George is handsomely executed; the veins in the back of his hands, and the folds of his stockings, in short the drapery in general, is happily executed. In one place of the Chancel is to be seen a statue alone on its back of the son of Constantine the Great, &c., &c.

The Chapterhouse, where the Bishops are installed, is one of the most magnificent octagons in the world.—In short, after having seen St. Paul's, the Cathedral of York will not fail to strike the stranger with astonishment.

Saunter down by the side of the river Ouse to the New Walk. Then take a view of the Castle with the round Tower, where the ordnance and ammunition, &c., were wont to be kept.—Return in the dusk to the inn, and sup with a Mr. Mariott, a curious talkative gentleman of Manchester, a sedate, superior gentleman, a Mr. Braddock of Macclesfield, and another gentleman whose name I did not hear mentioned.

Friday, 21st August. York.—This city has little trade; because no man can set up in business here without purchasing the freedom of the city, which is an expensive matter, and to beginners in business altogether unattainable. Something, I am told, is done here or at least may be done in the whip way. No vessels of any great consequence come up to the town. The city is surrounded with walls, and has double gates. The best point for viewing it is from the south-west as you come from Borrowbridge [Boroughbridge] to the bank of the river Ouse. Here the river, the walls of the city, its spires and towers, together with the Cathedral rising magnificent over all, exhibits a very picturesque and striking scene.

Leave York at half-past seven a.m., and pass over a long-extended heath, taking different names in different places according to the adjoining towns to which it belongs. About the sixth mile from York, pick up some plants of the *Gentiana Centaurium.* About the ninth mile from York, pass by on my right hand Housholm, an elegant Seat of Cholmondly, Esq.;[1] the ruins of Barboro' Castle on my left, belonging to the same. Arrive about eleven o'clock at Whitewell[2] Inn, under an heavy rain. Stop here and breakfast.—At one p.m. set out from Whitewell Inn, and come to the Gate leading to Castle Howard (Seat of the Earl of Carlisle).

Pass through a series of gates and well-dressed parks. Betwixt the third and fourth gate observe a grey-tailed squirrel crossing the road and climbing up the trees; it seemed to be a different species from those at Dunkeld. Betwixt the fourth and fifth gates, have an admirable view of the Castle and the park, with the woods, pyramids, temples and mausoleum. Come into the great avenue leading to Howard Inn, and enter at the fifth gate under a stone arch. On each side of the entrance a wall extends a great way to right and left, embrasured atop and terminated on each hand with a tower. Pass along the avenue in a straight line to Howard Inn, forming a fine object with a pyramid rising over the centre of the building, and coveting the arch through which the highway passes. The trees on each side of this stately avenue are disposed in little plantations of about sixteen or twenty large trees in each clump, separated from one another by an empty space of about a hundred

[1] 'Housham, N. Cholmley, Esq.' (Paterson's *Itinerary*).
[2] 'Whitwell.' Twelve miles from York (Paterson's *Itinerary*).

feet, through which empty space you have a delightful view of the Park and its environs. This disposition of the trees takes off from the tedious uniform dulness of a great avenue, where the trees are close and uninterrupted on each side of the traveller.

When you ascend to the gate-way at the Inn, through the arch you have a striking view of Marlborough Pillar,[1] placed at a distance in the centre of the avenue, which is continued in a

[1] [Footnote by the diarist.] Inscription on the north-west side of Marlborough Pillar:

If to perfection these plantations rise;
If they agreeably my halls surprise;
This faithful pillar will their age declare,
As long as time these characters shall spare.
Here then with kind remembrance read his name,
Who for posterity perform'd the same.
Charles the Third Earl of Carlisle,
Of the family of the Howards,
Erected a Castle where the old Castle of Henderskelf stood,
And called it Castle Howard.
He likewise made the plantations in this Park,
and all the out-works,
Monuments, and other plantations belonging
to the said Seat.
He began this work
In the year 1702,
And set up this inscription
In the year 1731.

Inscription on the south-east side of Marlborough Pillar:
Virtuti et fortunæ
Joannis Marlburiæ ducis,
Patriæ Europæq. defensoris,
Hoc saxum
Admirationi ac famæ sacrum,
Carolus Comes Carliol. posuit,
Anno Domini MDCCXIV.

straight line for about two miles beyond the inn. Put up at Howard Inn (Warwick's). Get a guide and go down to

CASTLE HOWARD.

This is altogether a princely place, and superior to any I have yet seen. A great part of the house is lately built, and the works are not yet finished. The style of the whole is simple but magnificent, and more extensive than I suppose most of the Palaces of Europe. The rooms are spacious and elegant, and the prospect of the park from each side of the Castle is fine beyond description.

Go in to the Gardens. Here is the first[1] pinery I ever saw, and upon the whole the best kept hot-houses. The vines most luxuriant; and here is what I never saw before, almond-trees, peaches, nectarines, etc., trained upon spars placed not as usual in a perpendicular but in a horizontal position, about two feet from the ground, and bearing abundance of rich fruit. Mr. Abel the gardener thinks this a good way.

From the Garden went next along the front of the Castle along the lawn by the statues to the Temple. This a most magnificent dome, finished entirely within with the most costly marble.

From the Temple proceed to the Mausoleum. The Mausoleum stands on a rising ground about a mile south from the Castle, and commands a

---

[1] As in previous instances, 'first' is probably used here with reference to degree, not time.

fine view of the bridge, the three ponds, the lawn, the castle, the park, the plantations, and different peeps of the country to a great distance. This is the Burying-place of the Family, and perhaps one of the most magnificent things of the kind in the world. It covers an acre of ground. A spacious Dome rises in the centre, its roof supported by twenty pillars, each pillar about twelve feet round and not less than fifty high. The floor of the dome within is laid with the finest variegated marble: here the funeral service is performed. All round the base of the dome within are placed niches for depositing the coffins, which when deposited are shut up and inscribed with the name of the person that lies there.

In this solemn scene there is indeed capacious room, sufficient for holding

'All the blood of all the Howards.'

A few of the niches only are shut up.

The Earl of Carlisle has here upwards of four hundred acres of mowing ground about the Castle, and the largest quantities of hay I ever saw. The park extends about four miles each way. There are vast varieties of venerable trees, finely disposed. Some of the oaks here upwards of twenty feet in circumference.

Everything about this place is in a style approaching to the sublime.

Leave Howard Inn after dinner and set out for Helmsley, fourteen miles to the north-west of Howard-Castle. About a mile north-east of the

Castle my Lord Carlisle is working excellent limestone with a coarse kind of coal brought up the Derwent. There is no burning coal in this country. For this coarse coal they pay just now at the landing-place at the rate of sixteen shillings the chaldron, thirty-two bushels. In the Park observe the *Pinguicula Lusitanica*. Arrive at the highest point of the ground at the northeast end of the great avenue : here stop and look back upon Castle Howard and its Entrance. Bid adieu to this great prospect, and descend the hill. A Castle in ruins on my right ; fine country before me. But the view clouded by an approaching storm.

Under a row of 'reverend elms' observe the following plants : *Origanum vulgare, Clinopodium vulgare, Marrubium vulgare, Campanula Trachelium*, &c. A cloud pours down a deluge upon me. Pass through a plain country, and approach the high grounds. Ascending the hill observe plants of *Verbascum thapsoides, Reseda Luteola*, &c.

Rain continues pouring without mercy; the roads run in streams. Night comes upon me in thick darkness as I approach Helmsley. Fall in with a man driving coals to Helmsley. He informs me there are no coals in this neighbourhood, save what they bring all the way from Malton, eighteen miles off, at the rate of eighteen shillings the chaldron.

Put up at Wilson's. A good comfortable fire in the kitchen; take this as the best room in the house. Get tolerably dry before supper. A gentleman from Ferrybridge, a friend of Sir John Ramsden, joins my company, with whom converse till eleven o'clock. Then go to bed.

Saturday, 22nd August. Helmsley.—Rise at seven a.m., and go up to see the Old Castle. It has been a stately pile, surrounded by a double moat, and strongly barricaded with gates. The walls are in some places nine feet thick: vast masses of them are tumbling down into the moats. It was demolished, like many other respectable Castles, by the rude hand of Oliver Cromwell.

From the Old Castle direct my morning walk to Duncombe Hall, a beautiful Seat of Charles Brinsly Duncombe, Esq.[1] It stands about half a mile above the village of Helmsley. Its principal front is towards the west, where it looks into a large deer-park finely stocked with deer, and surrounded with thick woods. From the deer-park the spectator has a charming view of the country and the adjacent moors far and wide. On the east front of the house, within the pleasure ground, is the bowling green, from which to the right and the left is extended, in a semicircular form, one of the finest green walks that can possibly be conceived. It stretches along a high bank and has a fine terrace running parallel with it and sloping down all the way to

---

[1] 'Duncomb Park, T. Duncomb, Esq.' (Paterson's *Itinerary*).

through Great Britain in 1795   129

the skirts of the wood that adorns the face of the bank. In the den below runs a pretty romantic stream with dashes of water and cascades, making a rushing noise upon the air, heard solemn through the dark and silent grove. This green walk is terminated on either hand with a neat temple which, like the mansion-house and the offices, are all of the simple Doric order of architecture. The garden lies low and warm, at a considerable distance to the north of the house, near the village of Helmsley. Here are nice green- and hot-houses, kept in excellent order. The paintings in Duncombe Hall are by some connoisseurs preferred to those at Castle Howard. But Duncombe is a miser, and unlike his brother the member of Parliament for the country [county]. This estate was purchased by one of the present proprietor's ancestors, who was connected with James VII., and retained the King's money in his hands after the Abdication.

After breakfast leave Helmsley, and take the hilly country for sixteen miles up the narrow valley of Billsdale, all the property of Squire Duncombe. He has a vast extent of moors in this neighbourhood, extending forty or fifty miles, abounding with the common grouse. I am informed the black grouse are found, though not in plenty, upon the property of Sir W. Fowlis, of Ingleby Manor, in this neighbourhood.

About sixteen miles north of Helmsley leave the hilly country and come down upon the plain.

Arrive about four p.m. at Stocksley, twenty miles north of Helmsley, after having been drenched to the skin by heavy rains. Much of the corn is laid flat by the rains of this day and last night.— In this long, high stage of steep and rough road (the most difficult I have yet passed over in England), there is no resting-place, save a little alehouse or two near the head of Billsdale, where I stopped to give Cally a mouthful of hay, for they had no corn, and myself a mouthful of ale.

In this tract I observed plenty of *Empetrum nigrum, Betonica officinalis, Epilobium angustifolium, Solidago virga - aurea,* &c. On coming down from the hilly region (Sir W. Fowlis's on my right), you leave on your left hand a tract of mountain somewhat resembling the Lomond Hills of Fife, but not so high, stretching from east to west about four miles south of Stocksley[1] [Stokesley]. At the top of the hill, where you first come in view of the plain, the prospect is very agreeable; the country before you for thirty or forty miles appears all plain as a bowling-green, and decorated as a garden. On coming down into the plain, I observed by the wayside a good deal of *Gentiana Centaurium,* growing with the *Ononis spinosa,* &c.

On arriving at Stocksley, a considerable village here, find it the weekly market. A good number

---

[1] The Cleveland Hills would seem to be here indicated, with the peaks of Botton Head and Loose Howe, to represent the West and East Lomonds in Fife.

of country people and farmers in the town; but little grain is sold here. They sold some here to-day at nine shillings a bushel; so that it seems it has not yet fallen here as in the South. The hay everywhere much damaged by the rains; a great deal of it still in the fields. No corn cut down in this part of the country. They do not expect harvest here for three weeks to come. Upon the whole this season seems to be, at a medium, three weeks later than last, and this over all England. Leave Stocksley at half-past five p.m., and set out for Stockton.

About four or five miles north of Stocksley, on the way to Stockton, the ground rises gradually to a considerable elevation. Here the rain ceasing and the clouds dispersing, I enjoy one of the most pleasing prospects the Island can boast of. A romantic range of mountains, which I had now left about seven miles beyond [? behind] me, stretches west several miles and terminates abruptly in the plain. To the east, on my right hand, another and a smaller range, but with one remarkable mountain (Roseberry Topping) of a pyramidal form towering 'proudly eminent' above the rest, extends north about eight or ten miles and then slopes downward towards the coast. On the west a broad expanse of plain country embellished with every ornament that the hand of art can bestow upon it, and this vast plain fringed by the summits of high mountains seen at the distance of fifty and sixty miles. On the north and north-west the county of Durham rising by a gentle ascent from the banks of the river Tees, seemingly for twenty or thirty miles, and also decorated in the highest manner, and terminated by the tops of mountains. In the bottom of the rich flat country before me, the Tees itself (town of Stockton on the north bank of the river) winding in sweet meanders through the vale, widening towards the north-east into a capacious Bay, and losing itself in the German Ocean; with the distant coast towards Hartlepool, and a number of sails descried at different distances from the shores to the very verge of the horizon. The setting sun darting from his broadened orb his inclined [or 'unclouded'] rays over the whole. On such a scene as this the mind of the contemplative traveller delights to dwell. A mild, sweet, and tranquil evening brings me to Stockton.

Before you enter the town, you pass the Tees by an elegant bridge of five arches, where the river is seen winding delightfully along and forming islands in its course. On these islands and on the plains on each side of the river, groups of flocks and herds are seen amusing themselves in sportive maze.

'Now is the time
For those whom Reason and whom Nature charm
To steal themselves from the degen'rate crowd;
To tread low-thoughted pride beneath their feet;
And woo lone Quiet in her silent walks.'

CHAPTER IX.

Stockton—Durham—Newcastle—Morpeth—Alnwick Castle—Chillingham and its White Cattle—The Cheviot Hills—Flodden Field—Across the Border.

SUNDAY, 23rd August. Stockton.—It is a beautiful town, consisting chiefly of one straight street about a quarter of a mile long and about sixty or seventy yards broad, with the market-place and town-hall in the middle of it: a few small streets cross it at right angles, running down to the side of the river. Little trade is carried on here; there is a fine corn country all round, and a great export of corn from this place. The river Tees constitutes the wealth of the place. The corn sold here lately at twenty-four shillings the bushel. The river abounds with a flat fish resembling a flounder or small turbot; they call it the plaice. It tastes somewhat like the flounder, but is whiter in its colour and not quite so juicy and delicate. Ships of one hundred and twenty tons come up here, and a ship of eight hundred tons was lately built here.

Leave Stockton at seven a.m., and set out for Durham. The *Poa aquatica* grows plentifully in the ditches about Stockton. A little to the north of this place I observed a fine field of turnips *drilled*, a very rare sight in England except about the Borders.[1]—Pass through a rich country; hedges and hedgerows of elms, &c., poplars, &c. The country rises by slow degrees, affording a grand prospect on each side; the morning very fine. Arrive half-past nine o'clock at Sedgefield,[2] where stop and breakfast.

Sedgefield is a neat village, situated in the heart of a fine, rich corn country. The rector here (Barrington) has a living of fourteen hundred pounds a-year. He officiates himself with one curate, and is esteemed a good preacher and a good farmer. He is a nephew of the Bishop of Durham.—From Sedgefield to Durham eleven miles. No waste ground all the way; every inch inclosed with hedge and plantation, and cultivated in the highest style. Lime and coal in abundance. See by the way-side plenty of *Malva moschata*, &c.

Approach to Durham about two p.m. The view of the cathedral, as you come in to the bank of the river Weir at the bridge, is picturesque and romantic in the highest degree. The great tower has a striking resemblance to the steeple of Dundee: the other two towers at the west

---

[1] See remarks on this subject, p. 119, footnote.
[2] About ten miles from Stockton, *viâ* Norton.

end of the minster put one a little in mind
of those at the west end of the minster of
York.

The river here has a curious serpentine course
through high, steep woody banks. Before you
enter the city you pass the river over two bridges,
and before you leave the city you pass it again
over a third bridge, where you see a fourth a little
above. The city itself is crowded along the
winding bank of the river. The streets and
entries are in many places steep and awkward
and inconvenient. The convenience of the *water*
has tempted the people to build it in this manner.
The grounds about Durham are highly beautiful ;
wherever you wander in the vicinity of the city
you are charmed with the sight of wood and
water.

Go to the Cathedral of Durham, and attend
the afternoon service. The organs with their
accompaniments admirably calculated to heighten
the devotion.

The Cathedral of Durham is a large, stately,
gothic structure, with vast appendages. But, to
one who has so lately seen the Minster of York,
it will not appear so striking as otherwise it
might.—After hearing the chanting in Cathedral,
take a walk about the place and view its dimensions.

The first public walk about the city is the
Prebend's Walk, along the bank of the Weir,
towards the race-ground. The ground here lets

at four pounds the acre. This walk is much frequented by the gentry of the city; it is finely sheltered on the north, and the river winds sweetly along in the valley below.

Leave Durham at six p.m., and set out for the North, along the great North Road. After passing the north bridge, you ascend a steep hill and lose sight at once of the city. For some miles proceed along a large common, now about to be enclosed and cultivated. Leave the common, and have on the right hand a fine prospect of Lumley Castle, the Seat of Lord Scarborough, a large square pile, with a square tower embrasured at each corner. The park extensive and well-wooded; some very large oaks, &c., here.

Arrive in the dusk at Chester-le-Street, nine miles south from Newcastle,[1] and put up there all night. Sup with a very intelligent gentleman of Yorkshire, on his way from Scotland. Converse with him till eleven p.m., and then go to bed.

Monday, 24th August. Newcastle.—Leave Chester-le-Street at seven a.m., and proceed over a hilly coal-country till we come within three miles of Newcastle. Here from a rising ground have a fine view backwards towards Durham. Advance a little farther to the grindstone and coal-works up the hill, and enjoy a delightful

---

[1] More correctly, eight miles from Newcastle. The distance from Durham to Chester-le-Street is six miles, so that the diarist had travelled twenty-seven miles that day.

prospect of the coast and the ocean. Proceed a little farther, and have a view of Newcastle below you. Come down upon the village of Gateshead. Cross the Tyne, and arrive in Newcastle to breakfast. Newcastle a very ugly, large, irregular town. The river Tyne, here separating the Counties of Durham and Northumberland, seems to be scarcely as broad as the Tay at Perth. The bridge has nine arches. Great coal trade the staple of this town. Ships of two masts come up here, but not in great numbers. Vessels of considerable burden are built here, but not so large as those built at Shields.

After breakfast take a walk to the Quay. Thence up the north side of the river to the Northumberland Glass Warehouse, through a narrow, dirty street, if it may be so called, as most of the streets here, except Dean Street and Pilgrim Street, are. Arrive at the west gate by the river side (here is the east termination of the Picts' Wall[1]). Go out to the Cast Metal and Brass foundery, &c. Walk up the north bank of the Tyne to get a prospect of this nasty, sooty, smoky chaos of a town. The view[s] of the river, the bridge, and the boats sailing down with the tide, with the country on each side of the river to the west, are, however, not unpleasant. The bank here abounds with the *Scrophularia*

[1] Hadrian's Wall was so known in Scotland at that date, if not also in Northumberland.

aquatica; and here also I observed some plants of *Oenanthe crocata,* &c.

From the top of the north bank, about half a mile above the bridge, you have perhaps the best prospect of the place. This *dark hulk* of a town is here seen on your left hand rising abruptly from the north side of the river; the bridge with all its arches appears before you, connecting Newcastle with the village of Gateshead on the Durham side, which also rises steep and sudden from the south side of the river. Through the arches of the bridge you descry the shipping for a great way down the river, which winds away out of sight under steep banks. The new church, resembling St. Andrew's Church in Dundee, here appears to great advantage in the face of the background, which rises to a considerable height, cultivated to the top, and adorned with enclosures, hedge-rows, trees, villas, &c.

After viewing the most considerable streets and lanes of the place, take a turn to St. Nicholas' Church and view its inside. Nothing very striking about it;—nor indeed about this place. The inhabitants here, like those of Sheffield, have in general got a tincture from the soot of coal-engines, founderies, glass-works, &c.—Return to the White Hart and dine; determined to leave this place, and if possible to be in the evening at Morpeth.

At four p.m. leave Newcastle and proceed to the fourth mile-stone, where pass on my right hand *Gossforth* (Brandling, Esq., Member of Parliament for the County. He is here represented as a good, generous, charitable man; and as having shewed himself so in a particular manner during the last severe winter). About the eighth mile-stone pass on my left hand *Blagdon* (Sir Matthew White Ridley). There is a pretty serpentine canal in the Park on the left hand, which seen through the trees as you pass along produces a very agreeable effect.

In the evening come to Morpeth.[1] The country hereabout remarkably well cultivated. The small river Wensbeck passes this town. The tide does not reach within five miles of the Borough. As you approach the town from the south you pass by a Castle in ruins belonging to the Carlisle family. The borough of Morpeth is entirely at the command of the Earl of Morpeth. It is said here it costs him every year two thousand pounds; consequently he ought to have something indeed to expect from it.

The oats here are sold at present for twenty-five shillings the boll of six Winchester bushels, here called the *old* boll. At Newcastle, and to the south of this for a great way, the *new* boll is used, viz. two bushels.—The crops around this place admirably good. The grain everywhere begins to fall in its price. Heaven send good weather and a good harvest!

[1] Fourteen miles from Newcastle. The day's ride from Chester-le-Street to Morpeth was thus twenty-three miles.

Tuesday, 25th August. Morpeth stands in a pleasant but low and obscure situation on the north side of the river. It contains about four thousand people. The houses are low, and many of them old, and thatched. The streets are very rough, and stand much in need of new paving. The country around is very beautifully wooded, and the surface of the ground agreeably diversified.

Leave Morpeth after breakfast and proceed towards Alnwick. For some miles the ground rises by a gentle ascent. At the third milestone come in view of the ocean. A calm, mild morning :—the sun gilds the surface of the deep, and the white sail steals stately over the waves.

Advancing a little to the north, the summits of the Northumbrian mountains lift their heads at a distance on the left, while for several miles you see on the right hand the blue expanse of the German Ocean stretching from Tynemouth north towards Coquet isle. The country slopes gradually towards the shore for eight or ten miles, and abounds with every sort of grain.

Come in to the banks of the river Coquet at Felton, ten miles from Morpeth and nine from Alnwick. Pass the river, which here winds beautifully between steep wooded banks. On the left hand as you approach to the bridge is Felton Hall, formerly belonging to the Witheringtons, now to Riddell, Esq.[1]

---

[1] 'Felton Park, Riddell, Esq.' (Paterson's *Itinerary*).

Stop at Felton for an hour and refresh my horse. The country very pleasant here. Leave Felton. On my left hand, Lisle, Esq. A little forward on my right Grieve, Esq., his *Folly* as it is called. It seems Mr. Grieve's folly consisted in improving his country. For several years he employed dozens of day-labourers in paring,[1] burning, draining, &c.; and out of moors, mires, and rushes, he raised farmsteads, plantations and enclosures of the first sort, making a paradise of a desert. Poor man, he died suddenly and unexpectedly in London some time ago; and all his improvements are the property of a West Indian nabob, whose name I have forgot, and whose character I was not at the pains to enquire into. But that is of no consequence; he may be a very eminent and a very worthy man for all that.

A vast many fine lime-works in this neighbourhood. About the thirteenth mile from Morpeth the road rises to a considerable elevation, from whence have a prospect again of the sea and the coast. You see Coquet isle and its Light-house on your right hand at about eight miles' distance. The island lies about three miles from the mainland.

Betwixt Morpeth and Alnwick, observed in several places plenty of *Betonica officinalis;* in some places, *Oenanthe crocata;* near the bridge of

[1] That is, removing the turf. In some parts of Scotland the expression 'flaying the muir' is used.

Felton, some plants of *Hieracium umbellatum ;* betwixt Felton and Alnwick, *Sisymbrium amphibium, S. Sophia;* in one place *Hypericum Androsaemum;* in another place, *Euphorbia Characias,* &c.

Arrive at Alnwick about five p.m. After dinner, go to the Castle, the old family-seat of the Earl Percys of Northumberland. The present Duke in bad health; he has been for some years past at Lisbon, is now come home, and resides at Zion-house near Richmond on the Thames.

A Mr. Kirk, a favourite old soldier of the present Duke, whom his Grace has appointed superintendent of the Castle, conducts me through the outworks, and shews and explains them to me in the most sensible and satisfactory manner. He seems to be a man possessed of much knowledge of the world, has fought in many battles, and discovers learning, penetration, and intelligence beyond what might naturally be expected from a sergeant. There are several curious pieces of antiquity here. A great number of old arms, coats of mail, helmets, &c. He shewed me, among many others, the helmet of the famous *Henry Hotspur.* There are here also some very curious Roman and Grecian antiques.—I went down into the Dungeon, where the prisoners used to be confined of old. An iron grate is lifted up, and a trap-ladder leads you down eleven or twelve steps into a place where no ray of light ever penetrated. My vanity was considerably flattered indeed when Kirk told me that the good and benevolent, the Great Howard, had been there before me.

When Kirk had shewn me the outworks, he conducted me to the gate of the inner castle itself, and there recommended me to a lady-servant[1] who shewed me all the apartments: First, the bed-rooms; second, the saloon; third, the dining-room; fourth, the drawing-room; fifth, the parlour or breakfasting-room; sixth, the Library; seventh, the Chapel, where there is a noble marble monument, placed under the great painted window, to the memory of the late Duchess of Northumberland by Hugh, the late Duke, who repaired the whole works here both outer and inner.—The furniture here is superb; the floors are all either wainscot or a hard kind of plaister, solid and durable as marble; the ceilings, &c., are magnificent, and everything done in a truly gothic style which greatly suits the building without.

After seeing this ancient and venerable place, take a walk through the Park, by the side of the river Ale, which winds sweetly along at the foot of the bank under the Castle. A noble bridge of three large arches here bestrides the river, and the effigy of a huge lion stands grinning upon the parapet of the middle arch. The view of Alnwick Castle from the different points of the Park, which

---

[1] This term, which has a curiously modern sound, no doubt indicates a woman of the 'Mrs. Rouncewell' type, to whom such a term may not inaptly be given.

is about seven miles round, is sublime. About two and a half miles east of the Castle, the Duke has built an artificial ruin on the top of a high precipice, whence Alnwick may be viewed to great advantage. About a mile to the west of the Castle stands a high pillar on the top of a hill, from whence also the view is noble. The principal view is from the north-east, from near Malcolm the Third's Cross.[1]

On the turrets and embrasures of the Castle all round are placed huge statues of old Warriors in different attitudes. At a little distance they seem to be alive and employed in defending the works. In short, this Castle is altogether done in a singularly Gothic style, and has altogether a singular and striking appearance.

In the evening, on the parade before the gates of the Castle, see Colonel Blake's Regiment drawn up. They have a tolerable Band of music per-

[1] [Footnote by the diarist.] In the Park. Inscription on the north-west side of Malcolm's Cross :
'Malcolm III., King of Scotland,
Besieging Alnwick castle,
Was slain here
November 13, ANNO MXCIII.'

On the opposite side :
'King Malcolm's cross,
Decayed by time,
Was restored by his
Descendant Elizabeth,
Duchess of Northumberland,
1774.'

On the south-west, *The Lion.*
On the north-east, *The Thistle.*

formed by blacks and Indians;[1] but as for the soldiers they make but a sorry appearance, consisting for the most part of mere boys and *old men,* the outcasts of the London jails, &c., poor, decrepit, nerveless, worn-out debauchies. How exceedingly unlike those old Northumbrian heroes whose very statues now look down from these walls upon them with pity and contempt!

Wednesday, 26th August. Alnwick.—In the morning leave Alnwick and ascend an eminence: here the Earl's Mount, as it is called, appears to great advantage on the West hand. On its summit is raised a huge Pillar by the late Duke. This is a very curious piece of architecture. By a turnpike of a singular kind within the pillar you ascend nearly a hundred feet. At the top of this is a battlement, where you go out and walk round,

[1] With regard to these 'blacks and Indians,' some further information seems desirable. If this was one of the East India Company's regiments, they were probably East Indians. On the other hand, it is possible that they were simply gypsies from Rothbury and Coquetdale. As at the present day in Hungary, the gypsies of the British Islands were formerly notable musicians; and it is certainly the case that one celebrated Northumbrian gypsy, who came of a family of hereditary musicians, was 'regimental piper in the Northumberland Militia' not many years before the date of this Diary, prior to which period he had been retained by the Duchess of Northumberland as her special piper. [See Mrs. E. R. Pennell's article, 'A Gypsy Piper,' in the *Journal of the Gypsy Lore Society,* vol. ii., No. 5, January, 1891. For some remarks on black men as musicians in British regiments, see also a note by the present annotator in *Notes and Queries* (Series VII., vii. 448) and subsequent comments (Series VII., vii. 517; and Series VII., viii. 32, 97, and 237).]

having an amazingly grand view of Alnwick Castle, the town, and the country all round. High up above the battlement is placed a curious *grate*, on which a bonfire is kindled on extraordinary occasions.

About four miles north of Alnwick you have a distinct view of the Cheviot on your left, the highest mountain in Northumberland. The prospect of the ocean on the right obscured greatly to-day by a sort of hazy vapour hanging over it. Have at intervals, however, a view of Bamburgh Castle, situated on a peninsula, a curious old ruin. The Fern isles and Holy island may be seen here. About four miles south of Belford, pass by on my left hand Selby, Esq.[1] As you come within a mile or two of Belford, have a fine view of Belford-hall (Dickson,[2] deceased), delightfully situated on the declivity of a hill, and finely embosomed in wood. The village of Belford stands a little to the west of the house, lower down towards the vale.

Arrive at the Bell Inn about eleven a.m. The day exceedingly warm and sunny. The hay-harvest going on briskly; but no corn cut down yet in any part of this country. Fine sheep of the Culley's breed in the parks in this neighbourhood. Excellent sheep-farms here.

[1] Evidently the 'New-hall, Bacon, Esq.,' of Paterson's *Itinerary*, published ten years earlier.
[2] The 'Dixon, Esq.,' of Paterson's *Itinerary*. The diarist, as a Scotchman, naturally spells the name in the Scotch fashion.

Betwixt Alnwick and Belford observed no particular plants by the way-side except *Lythrum Salicaria, Plantago media, Geranium pratense,* and a few plants of *Betonica officinalis* in one place only.—Price of oats just now at Belford twenty-five shillings a boll of six Winchester bushels, equal to four Scotch firlots.

Have an interview here with Mr. and Mrs. Richardson, and Mr. and Mrs. Duncan and Miss Stewart of Urard [Perthshire], returning from the Lakes. After parting with them, have another interview with Mr. Wishart of Edinburgh, returning also from the Lakes.

Set out in the afternoon for Chillingham, six miles across a high, swampy, heathy country, from the top of which have a view of the coast, Bamburgh Castle, the Fern isles, Holy island, and the ocean. Here take my leave of the east coast of England, and set my face to the Cheviot mountains. Come down upon Chillingham, an old strong retreat of the Earl of Tankerville, situated on the west side of a high range of black, heathy hills, whereof the highest is Rosehill immediately above the Castle.

There being no inn in the village, the Rev. Dr. Thomas, the Vicar of the place, receives myself and horse, and entertains both with the most hospitable attentions. We may boast of our Scotch hospitality as we please, but I have repeatedly found hospitality in England too. Why should not one of the first of Christian

virtues reside in England as well as in Scotland?
—The Doctor an open-hearted, communicative
man. He accompanies me to shew me the object
of my excursion to this place, viz., the old Caledonian White Cattle, which the Goth Duke of
Queensberry has extirpated from Scotland,[1] and
which, I am told, are now to be seen nowhere in
the Island save in this very spot. Saw a large
drove of them, mixed with the fallow-deer, in a
park a little above Chillingham Castle. They
are all white except their ears, and a little under
the tail; have all nearly similar horns, erect and
beautiful; are pretty tall and thin on the limbs.
When you approach them they are shy and retire
from you frightened, but if you persevere chasing
them, and if they think you design to harass
them, they turn in a body against you and attack
you.

The Doctor shews me also the front of the
Castle. It is a piece of very thick, strong work,
built in the feudal times, when the borderers
were perpetually at war with one another, and
built their castles generally in dark, gloomy,
retired fastnesses.

Drink tea with the Vicar. He gives me the

---

[1] Although there is nowadays a herd of the old white
cattle preserved in the Duke of Hamilton's park at Cadyow,
the survivors of the original stock at that place were 'exterminated, from economical motives, about the year 1760.'
The Duke of Queensberry's herd at Drumlanrig shared a
like fate in 1780-1790. (See the *Proceedings of the Society
of Antiquaries of Scotland*, vol. ix., p. 601.)

history of his family. His son very unfortunate. Shews me a letter from the Duke of Portland, and another from the Bishop of Durham, relative to his son. Both these letters written in a very peculiar style. Mrs. Thomas a Scotch-woman from Fife.

Vicar shews me his garden and houses. A new kind of pease, rich and requiring no support. Promises to send me a specimen of them in autumn.

Part with this good, hospitable man, and set out across the hill. A fine evening, and a most beautiful setting sun. Cheviot a little to the westward of me: a blue-gray nightcap enwraps his black and lofty head. Come down the hill to the bank of the river at Wooler. The rays of the departed sun 'yet line with purple and with florid gold' the clouds disposed in thin horizontal strata over the northwest parts of the heavens. Pass the river. See here plenty of *Geranium cicutarium*, very luxuriant plants. Great banks of sand are here deposited on the plain, being brought down from the Cheviot mountains in the time of floods. Arrive at Wooler, where put up all night at the Sign of the Black Bull, on the east termination of the Cheviot hills.

Thursday, 27th August. Wooler, lying in the vicinity of green pastures and high mountains, enjoys a free and healthy air, for the sake of which, as well as of drinking the goat-whey, many people resort here during the summer, and spend six weeks and sometimes two months. The great severity of last winter killed the great part of the goats, and therefore fewer company are here at present than usual.

For twelve or fifteen miles along the foot of the Cheviot here, the hills are green and beautiful to their tops, feeding the finest fleeced sheep in the world. Their wool sometimes is sold at a guinea a stone-weight. They are much finer wooled than the sheep that feed higher up among the Cheviot mountains, which are mossy and benty[1] and heathy towards their summits. The Culley's breed of sheep are used here; small, white faces, and small delicate legs, with thick close fleeces as soft as any cotton. They are of a good size, and their mutton is esteemed very good.

Much corn grows here in the valleys, owing greatly no doubt to the limestone which is burnt hereabout in great quantities. The country in general, however, seems to be particularly calculated for hay and pasturage. Here as well as about Chillingham many small farms are turned into one large farm by a rich man over-bidding all poorer neighbours whenever their leases are out. This is a system much practised in other places as well as in this; and how far it may eventually prove hurtful to a country by depriving it of, what must be the strength and support of

---

[1] That is, full of bogs, and covered chiefly with *bent* or coarse wild grass.

any country, its *inhabitants*, is a question. Many parts of the Highlands of Scotland are now greatly depopulated by this plan; though it may be said the inhabitants are better employed in other places, where they are taught habits of useful industry, and so forth.

In Whitsunbank, betwixt Wooler and Chillingham, is held on Whitsunday, yearly, the greatest sheep and cattle fair in this country.

Leave Wooler at eleven a.m., and pass along the east base of the Cheviot, 'where erst with hound and horn Earl Percy took his way.' On my right hand a fine, flat, rich corn country lying on each side of the river Till, which, descending from the higher grounds, here receives a number of small streams from the Cheviot hills. These streams, meeting in the vale, take the name of Till, which runs north through a fertile country and falls into the Tweed.

At half-past twelve o'clock, come towards the scene of the Battle of Flodden. Here musing alone, the melancholy remembrance comes over my soul of that day so fatal to Scotland, to her king, and to his nobles! This the mournful scene of *The Flowers of the Forest*—' all faded away'!

The Battle-bush, as it is yet called, is not above half a mile to the left-hand of the road leading from Wooler to Cornhill.

Flodden-hill, where the Scottish army are said to have been posted, is now covered with artificial wood. Honey Laws' hill, where King

James the Fourth's men are said to have taken their stand before the engagement, is a little to the westward. On this hill are still to be seen green circular mounds and entrenchments; here is also the King's-chair, as it is still termed, cut out of the rock somewhat in the form of a chair; and here likewise the King's-bason, cut also out of the solid stone, where the King of the Scots is said to have sat and washed himself. But upon the surface of the ground hereabouts few memorials remain, few indeed of that memorable action. The country here all round exhibits at this day a very different and a far more pleasing spectacle. The plough has obliterated the graves of the Scottish and English heroes; and rich grain now waves over the hills where formerly waved the banners of hostile nations, now, thank Heaven! hostile no more.

A peasant here told me he had in his house a cannon-ball, found in his wife's father's time under the furrow of the plough, near the scene of the battle. He told me the bullet weighs about eighteen pound. Many weapons of war were dug up hereabouts at different times.

[Here follow some further statements relating to Flodden, obviously obtained from historical writers. The diary then continues thus:]

After leaving this neighbourhood, pass on till I come to Asky-hall, Askey, Esq.[1] It stands on the

---

[1] Read 'Pallinsburn Hall, Askew, Esq.' (Paterson's *Itinerary*).

north of the public road, on a bold eminence. Below it, in the hollow, is a curious pond or mire, cut into different canals, and abounding with the *Scirpus lacustris*, *Typha latifolia*, and other aquatic plants.

George Culley, so deservedly famed over all Britain, farms a great part of the lands here. I passed through the midst of his farms, and have seen nothing equal to them in Scotland or in England. His hedges are trimmed in the neatest manner; his enclosures are all of a good size, and perfectly regular. His soil is dry and warm and early, and richly manured with lime, which abounds in his neighbourhood. His sheep, horses, cows, are all the very best breed of England; and disposed in parks [*i.e.*, meadows or pasture-fields], each sort by themselves. His harvest is already begun; and his crops of oats, barley, vetches, pease, beans, rye, wheat, hay, &c., are most luxuriant. He drills his turnips in general, though he has a few fields in the broadcast for his sheep. His farms here are well worth going a hundred miles to see.

After leaving his farms at Asky-hill, proceed towards Cornhill, and come in view of the river Tweed, gliding in gentle meander by Wark Castle down to Coldstream-bridge; the Merse, Tweeddale, with the hills about Melrose, &c., in the background, here make a grand and beautiful appearance.

At Cornhill, come in upon my last year's tract.

Pass the Tweed at Coldstream-bridge, which here divides the two Kingdoms. Five stately arches bestride the stream, besides a small arch up on the bank on each side to receive the water in the time of a high flood. The bridge of Coldstream somewhat resembles the bridge of Perth in its architecture. A pier of large stones runs across the Tweed, immediately below the bridge, to deaden the current at the foundation of the bridge. This layer of stones produces a rushing of the water that has an agreeable effect on the ear as you pass the bridge.

Arrive at half-past two o'clock p.m. at the Black Bull Inn in Coldstream, and dine in Scotland. The harvest here about eighteen or twenty days later than it was here last year.

CHAPTER X.

Kelso—Mr. William Dawson—Tweedside and its Memories
—Peebles—Mid-Lothian—Return to Edinburgh.

THURSDAY, 27th August. — From Coldstream have a delightful evening ride up the north bank of the Tweed all the way to Kelso. No farming can possibly exceed the farming of this country, on both sides of the Tweed. In England it is in general much inferior. The harvest just begun here on both sides of the river, and the crops luxuriant as can be. Mr. Waldie sups with me at the Inn.

Friday, 28th August. Kelso.—Breakfast with Mr. Waldie, and have an agreeable *tête-à-tête* with Miss Euphemia Dawson in the forenoon. Dine at Mr. Waldie's, in company with Mr. Dawson, Miss Betty Dawson, Miss Archibald, niece of Mr. Dawson, Miss Thomson, and two young gentlemen. Pass the afternoon very agreeably. Sup at Mr. Waldie's.

Saturday, 29th August. Kelso.—Breakfast with Mr. Waldie. After breakfast went up to see the new bridge of Teviot, a piece of very neat architecture; three spacious arches; very fine white-coloured stone. Ride out with Captain Jefferies of Mainhouse. Dine at Frogden. Company, Mr. and Miss Dawson, young Mr. William Dawson, Mrs. Douglas, sister of Mr. Dawson, Miss Thomson, and two young Misses Waldie, Christian and Mary.

[At this point the entries become brief and concise; and, while containing little to attract the general reader, they denote a period of keen interest in the diarist's life. That journeys end in lovers' meeting is what every wise man's son is supposed to know; and this journey did not, in that respect, differ from others. For although the traveller was a bachelor of mature years, he had become attracted, only the previous summer it would seem, by the charms of the Miss Euphemia Dawson, whose name here frequently recurs, and their engagement definitely took place on this occasion, to be followed by their marriage in the succeeding year. This lady was one of the numerous family of an agriculturist of considerable note in his day. Of him a full account may be seen in the *Scots Magazine* for 1815 (pp. 420-424); and, in addition to casual notices in agricultural magazines, there are similar references in *Chambers's Edinburgh Journal* (1836) and in Forsyth's *Beauties of Scotland*. The last-named work contains (vol. ii., pp. 74-77, Edinburgh, 1805) the following statements:

'While the agriculture of this county [Roxburghshire], and the greater part of Scotland, was in the state we have now described; while the cattle were few, and consequently the crops of grain contemptible, the whole face of this county and of its neighbourhood was speedily altered, in consequence of an event which at the time must have appeared of little importance, but which produced the happiest effects to the general agriculture of Scotland. William Dawson, Esq., then a very young man, and the son of a farmer of Roxburghshire, after receiving a liberal education, was sent by his relations into England for the purpose of obtaining a practical knowledge of the most approved English husbandry. He resided four years in the West Riding of Yorkshire, and one year in Essex, labouring with his own hands under respectable farmers, to whose care he had been committed in consequence of recommendations obtained from Scotland to persons of rank, under whom their farms were held. He returned to Roxburghshire in 1753, and immediately introduced the practice of the turnip husbandry, which he sowed in drills.' [The *Scots Magazine* account, evidently more accurate, states that Dawson 'was born at Harperton, in Berwickshire, of which his father was tenant'; that he began his revolutionary treatment on his father's farm, after his return from England; and that his success in turnip-culture dates from his occupation of the farm of Frogden, Roxburghshire, in 1759.] 'He was the first Scottish farmer who introduced the cultivation of turnip into the open field. . . . Mr. Dawson's fields soon became more fertile and beautiful than those around him. . . . The hinds who had once been in his service were sure to find employment; his ploughmen were in the utmost request; . . . and Mr. Dawson, independent of his own personal prosperity, had the satisfaction to live to see himself regarded, and hear himself called, the father of the agriculture of at least the south of Scotland.'

Omitting, then, those passages which relate to this tender period, we resume the narrative with the traveller's resumption of his journey.]

Friday, 4th September.—Musing in lonely melancholy mood, I wandered on regardless of my way. The day was delightful. The country was sweet. Tweed glided on in gentle meanderings on my left.

Pass Smellam tower,[1] high seated among rocks. About three o'clock in the afternoon, I found myself among the Ruins of the Abbey of Dryburgh.

[Here follows a description of Dryburgh Abbey, which it is unnecessary to quote. The journey is then resumed.]

Wander up the delightful banks of the Tweed. About Old Melrose,[2] the windings of the river and its banks are indescribably beautiful.

Pass the river Leader: fine view of Tod's house[3] above you on your right hand. This whole paradise of a country is one continued scene of classic ground; the scenes of those beautiful simple Scotch pastoral songs, so much and so justly admired by all the world.

A magnificent bridge (Stevens') of three stately arches, the central one a hundred and five feet wide, carries me across the Tweed about two miles below Melrose. The country here begins

---

[1] Smailholm Tower, six miles west-by-north of Kelso. Although it possesses many historical associations (it dates from the early part of the fifteenth century), its greatest interest to modern readers must be its association with Sir Walter Scott. Here it was that, as an infant, he was found lying on the grass, during a thunderstorm, 'clapping his hands at each flash, and shouting, "Bonny! bonny!"' And he afterwards made this the scene of his *Eve of St. John*, and again recalled its wild charms in the introduction to Canto Third of *Marmion*.

[2] Three miles down the Tweed from the more modern Melrose.

[3] ? Drygrange House.

to be hilly. The Eildon-hills form here grand objects on your left as you go up to Melrose Abbey.

At six in the afternoon arrive at Melrose. Riddle, Esq., has an elegant house on your right as you enter the town. Go immediately to view the finest ruin in Scotland; travellers say one of the finest in the known world.

[As the account of Melrose Abbey which is here given contains nothing specially important, it is omitted.]

Saturday, 5th September. Melrose.—Leave this place at eleven o'clock a.m. About two miles north-west of Melrose, pass the Tweed along a bridge of two lofty arches. About two miles further on come to the bank of Gala Water at Galashiels (Colonel Scott).[1] Proceed along the banks of this romantic stream till I come to Torwoodlee (Pringle, Esq.). This must be considered as one of the most delightful summer residences that can anywhere be seen, as long as verdant hills, warm woody banks, and winding streams are ranked among the first beauties of nature.

Here leave the straight road to Edinburgh, and take to the left towards Peebles. Ride along a hilly tract for a few miles, then come in again

[1] This casual reference makes one realize the sudden rise of Galashiels, now a town of over 17,000 inhabitants, and an important centre of 'tweed' manufacture since the beginning of this century. In 1795, however, it was a small village of hand-loom weavers, and the diarist thought it sufficient to merely note the name of the laird.

to the pastoral banks of the Tweed, which a little to the south, near Selkirk, receives the Etterick, which last receives the *Yarrow* that gives immortality to Logan :

'Thy braes were bonny, Yarrow stream,' etc.[1]

Pass by Askysteel (Colonel Russell),[2] situated on the west bank of the river. Continue winding up the river towards the north. Pass by an old Castle belonging to Lord Elibank,[3] whence his title. Travel slowly on, the day delightful and sunny. Here Tweed begins to narrow his dale, and the hills rise in bold angles on each side of the river. No reaping here as yet, though the crop looks well; the country is rather late, being high among the hills. See some good fields of barley, and oats, and pease, and vetches, along the sides of the river. Come at last to Pirn (Horsburgh), covered with a clump of trees on your left as you approach to Innerleithing, a small village about six miles from Peebles.

Here is a woollen manufactory, driven by the small stream of the Leithing, which here falls into the Tweed. There is a good deal of spinning,

---

[1] From *The Braes of Yarrow*, by John Logan (1748-1788).

[2] 'Ashiesteel. . . . Long a seat of the Russells, of Indian military fame, it was tenanted from 1804 to 1812 by their kinsman, Walter Scott, then Sheriff of Selkirkshire . . . and what is now a passage was both the dining and his writing room, in which were composed the *Lay of the Last Minstrel*, the *Lady of the Lake*, and *Marmion*, as well as about a third of *Waverley*' (*Ordnance Gazetteer of Scotland;* edited by Francis Hindes Groome).

[3] Alexander Murray, seventh Lord Elibank (1747-1820).

weaving, and dyeing wool here as well as at Galashiels and Melrose. In the neighbourhood of this village there is also a mineral spring (salt), resorted to by company in the summer months. Its virtues were discovered about twelve years ago, before the Traquair family left this neighbourhood.[1]

Traquair lies on the opposite side of the Tweed here, a great deal of fine wood about it. The haughs here are very beautiful and extensive. This, I am told, is the real scene of the old song of 'The Bush aboon Traquair,'[2] and not that at Dumfries [Troqueer] as some have imagined.

The black grouse have been killed in this neighbourhood, though they are now a very rare bird here. The common grouse are on the hills here. The Tweed is a fine fishing stream here; but the accommodations for strangers are very indifferent indeed—'' Tis true, 'tis pity!' &c. The wool is the staple commodity of this country. The sheep here are the hardy black-faced kind. The ground is a good deal in a state of nature in most places. The old leases are out upon the Traquair Estate here, and a considerable rise of rent is expected, perhaps three times higher than the old. Limestone is brought here from twelve miles off, and coal from a still greater distance. The sheep farmers suffered much here by the severity of last

---

[1] This 'spaw' is the original of Scott's 'St. Ronan's.'
[2] The beauty of which has been eclipsed in recent years by Professor Campbell Shairp's lovely modern version.

winter: in the lambing time many hundreds of the sheep gave way.

Leave Innerleithing at four in the afternoon. The hills are beautiful all round; 'they rejoice on every side.' The road takes a northerly direction; keeps still along the bank of the river, following its beautiful winding course. Blue slate is dug out of the hills a little to the north of the House of Traquair; but they are soft, and by no means durable. The most valuable blue slate of this country are brought from Stouba [Stobo], about six miles south-by-west of Peebles.

About a mile beyond Innerleithing, pass by Cardronna [Cardrona] (Williamson, Esq.). It lies under a green hill with a great collection of stones on its top on the west bank of the Tweed. On the opposite bank is an old ruinous tower, with some apparent monuments of antiquity on the hill on the south side of it. Here farming is beginning to improve: beautiful fields slope gently towards the river. Turnip and potatoes thrive admirably here; and from the nature of the soil for many miles along the banks here, it would appear they cannot be too much encouraged.

Here fall in with a Mid-Lothian farmer, a sensible man, who accompanies me all the way to Peebles.

A few miles above Cardronna, on the same side of the river, lies Kyla [Kailyie], the Seat of Captain Campbell, one of the first of those numberless beauties that appear on the banks of the Tweed. On the side of the river opposite to it you pass by Horseburgh[1] Castle on your left;[2] then through one of the most delightful farms possible, Ash-hill [Eshiels] farm, belonging to Hay, Esq., of Hayston, brother-in-law to the present Duchess of Atholl.[3] This is truly a model of a farm. It is composed of a fine sloping bank facing the south, and ending in an extensive plain terminated by the Tweed. The road to Peebles runs through it, betwixt the bank and the plain: on each side of the road the parks [*i.e.*, pastures] are laid out in the most elegant manner, enclosed with fine young thriving hedges. The lime (though the carriage is long) here produces the most sudden and the most astonishing effects, the soil being everywhere dry and admirably fitted for it. The crops are proportionately luxuriant, and the harvest is just at hand.

As a proof of the excellence of the soil in general along the whole bank of this wonderful river, the hawthorn hedges, which in the lower parts of the country are planted *double*, but here *single*, thrive exceedingly, and grow perfectly regular without any breach.

[1] The correct spelling is 'Horsbrugh.'
[2] The diarist appears to have forded the Tweed above Cardrona.
[3] The laird of Hayston in 1795 was James Hay, M.D., who, in 1805, established his claim to the family baronetcy, dormant since 1683. It was his eldest son, however (Mr. John Hay, b. 1755, d. 1830), who was brother-in-law to the then Duchess of Atholl, he and the Duke of Atholl having married sisters, the daughters of James, sixteenth Lord Forbes (*Burke*).

Come to Peebles in the evening about six o'clock. It is a pretty, neat town, the capital of the County, situated on the north bank of the Tweed, and much resembles an English village. Its situation is indeed one of the most romantic that can be conceived.

The general course of the Tweed here is nearly from west to east. It passes under a very old and very narrow bridge of five equal arches. A large sandbank, accumulated immediately above the bridge, has thrown the whole weight of the current under the southmost arch; and unless the river is strongly banked on the south side above, there seems to be a danger of its leaving the bridge altogether.

To a spectator on the central arch of the Bridge, the river Tweed exhibits an appearance truly picturesque. About half a mile above the bridge the hills seem to entirely close, at Needpath [Neidpath], an old Castle of the Duke of Queensberry. Here the Tweed is seen rising as it were out of the base of the hills in one broad expansive fountain, which, stealing along in a smooth and placid winding towards the bridge, passes under it with a sudden sweep, and then gliding in gentle meanders by Hayston, is seen apparently sinking about two miles to the eastward under Horseburgh Castle, where the mountains again appear to close.

The scenery about Peebles would be by no means untempting to a judicious landscape painter. The view from the bridge down the river is very fine on each side. The view up the river is romantic in the first degree. Here the old Castle of Needpath forms a striking object, finely embosomed in the mountains whence the river seems to issue, which are half-way up covered with venerable old trees of different complexions, which this mischievous Duke is now occupied in cutting down, because he has no heir to leave them to. This man certainly enjoys a taste the most completely depraved of any man's alive. It is needless to remonstrate with him on the barbarity of his conduct; his unhallowed hand must be continually exercised in mangling every plantation he is heir to.[1]

Standing about two hundred yards above the Bridge on the south bank of the Tweed, and turning your face to the north, you see to the left hand Needpath in all its glory of scenery, before you the house of Honeyman, Esq., together with [the] Manse, both of them finely raised upon the north bank of the river; a little to the right of this the Ed[d]leston water coming down from the north, and falling into the Tweed at the west end of a peninsular eminence covered with black pines and crowned with the spire of the new church; beyond this, on the right, the town, the

[1] This Duke of Queensberry, already referred to by the diarist in similar terms (p. 148), was the notorious 'Old Q.' His treatment of the Neidpath woods drew forth from Wordsworth, who visited the place in 1803, the well-known lines beginning :

'Degenerate Douglas ! thou unworthy Lord !'

bridge, and the river, with the green hills rising beautifully in the background, on the face of which Mr. Grant's house, Smithfield, makes a delightfully conspicuous object.

Peebles is a cleanly little town, composed chiefly of one broad Street. The principal object in the way of building here is the new church, which seems to be rather pressed by a heavy-looking spire raised on its east end. The church, however, is a commodious piece of architecture, built of very good stone quarried in its neighbourhood. It is finely situated on the peninsular eminence above-mentioned, and forms the west boundary of the Broad Street.[1] On the top of this eminence is an excellent bowling-green adjoining the church.

A good deal of carpets are woven here, not for sale, but for gentlemen who employ the weavers for their private purposes. (Hawick is the principal carpet town of the South.) Peebles has also good schools for gentlemen's sons, who are educated here in considerable numbers. They have here fine air and fine room for exercise. It should therefore be encouraged as a proper place for a seminary of learning.

In sauntering along the banks of the Tweed this evening, fall in with an angler who shows me some trouts he had caught a little above the town.

[1] This name, casually given by the diarist, is not the actual name of the main street of Peebles. 'It was formerly the "Hie¦Gait," then High Street,' writes the Rev. Dr. Williamson, author of *Glimpses of Peebles* (1895).

It is a broad-shouldered well-formed fish, of a good size and excellent flavour. He had caught some pars, too, the largest I have ever seen. The trouts and eels in the Edleston river here are said to be superior to those of the Tweed.—Sup on pars from the Tweed.

Sunday, 6th September. Peebles.—Leave this in the morning, and direct my course northward along the east bank of the Edleston water. The crops rich on each side of the narrow vale, and the harvest in some places begun.

Ascending by the side of the Edleston brook, stop frequently and look back towards Peebles and the charming hills on each side of the Tweed. About two miles north of Peebles, the sweet scene vanishes from my sight.

About two miles north of Peebles, pass by Pringlety [*read* 'Cringletie'] (Colonel Murray).[1] It is beautifully situated on the west bank of the Edleston brook, which meanders sweetly through the little vale below. The house is well sheltered with wood, and the hills beyond 'lift their green heads to the sky.'

About a mile and a half to the north of Pringlety, on the same side of the bank, and similarly situated, lies Dairnhall [Darnhall], the Seat of Lord Elibank. A broad avenue of lime-trees leads your eye to the house as you pass along the turnpike road.

[1] Of this family came the eminent judge, James Wolfe Murray (1760-1836), who was raised to the bench with the title of Lord Cringletie.

After this, mount the higher grounds that separate the county of Peebles from Mid-Lothian. Heavy rain. Come in sight of the whole range of the Pentland hills, and Mid-Lothian lying at their feet. The clouds clear up. On your left hand here have a fine view of The Whim (Lord Chief Baron's),[1] embosomed in wood, on the south edge of the plain-country below you.

Stop at Howgate, where enter Mid-Lothian. Howgate lies about a mile and a half south-east of Sir John Clark's of Pennycuik. Now Arthur's Seat and Salisbury Crags appear in sight.

Leave Howgate at half-past three o'clock in the afternoon. Come down upon Mid-Lothian, and pass the river Esk between Auchindenny (Captain McKenzie) on my right hand and Greenlaw (Caddel, Esq.), on my left. The river here winds among steep woody banks, and the scenery around is exceedingly romantic.

Within four or five miles of the Capital, leave the great turnpike road, and strike across the country to the left towards the foot of the east end of the Pentland hills. Come in view of Mortonhall (Trotter, Esq.). Join the Linton road at the east end of the Pentlands. Here look back upon Lothian. Little harvest here as yet; though the crop in general looks well, and far advanced to maturity.

Here turning your eye east-by-north, you see at

[1] James Montgomery of Stanhope, 1721-1803; appointed Lord Chief Baron of the Court of Exchequer in 1775, and created a baronet in 1801, on his retirement from the bench.

the distance of about twenty-four miles in a straight line North Berwick Law rising like a huge pyramid, and flinging from its north side the mighty rock that forms the Bass island. The continent of East Lothian appears stretching north from this into the shining Firth of Forth, beyond which appears the East Nook of Fife in the verge of the horizon.

Proceed northwards to Peter Plenderleith's farm. Here some fields of barley are cut down.

In descending, just at the point where the road goes off to your right towards Braid Hermitage, you see before you the romantic rocks of Braid, Arthur's Seat and Salisbury Crags, the City of Edinburgh with its Castle, and the fine country extending from the Pentlands to the Forth; in the middle of the scene the broad firth of Forth with its islands; in the background the coast of Fife with the distant high hills of Largo Law, the Lomonds, &c.; all taken together forming a scene which, if not in beauty at least in sublimity, excels perhaps anything of the kind to be seen in the Southern Kingdom.

Approach slow to the Metropolis; the western sun illuminating the whole scene, and happily presaging a fine harvest day to-morrow.

THE END.

Elliot Stock, 62, Paternoster Row, London.

www.ingramcontent.com/pod-product-compliance
Lightning Source LLC
Chambersburg PA
CBHW020253170426
43202CB00008B/347